REFLECTIVE PRACTICE TO IMPROVE SCHOOLS

To Barb Vallejo and Jane Stevenson, our extraordinary reflective practice partners. Thanks for all the learning!

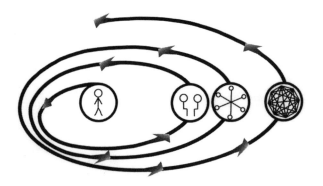

REFLECTIVE PRACTICE TO IMPROVE SCHOOLS

An Action Guide for Educators

Jennifer York-Barr • William A. Sommers
Gail S. Ghere • Jo Montie
Foreword by Arthur L. Costa

CORWIN PRESS, INC.
A Sage Publications Company
Thousand Oaks, California

For information:

Corwin Press, Inc.
A Sage Publications Company
2455 Teller Road
Thousand Oaks, California 91320
E-mail: order@corwinpress.com

Sage Publications Ltd.
6 Bonhill Street
London EC2A 4PU
United Kingdom

Sage Publications India Pvt. Ltd.
M-32 Market
Greater Kailash I
New Delhi 110 048 India

Printed in the United States of America

Library of Congress Cataloging-in-Publication Data

Reflective practice to improve schools: An action guide for educators /
by Jennifer York-Barr ... [et al.].
   p. cm.
   Includes bibliographical references (p.   ).
   ISBN 0-7619-7762-7 (cloth)
   ISBN 0-7619-7763-5 (paper)
1. Learning, Psychology of. 2. Self-knowledge, Theory of. 3.
School improvement programs.   I. York-Barr, Jennifer, 1958-   .
LB1060 R395 2001
370.15'23—dc21

                                               00-012739

This book is printed on acid-free paper.

                   04 05 06 10 9 8 7 6

Acquiring Editor:	Rachel Livsey
Corwin Editorial Assistant:	Phyllis Cappello
Production Editor:	Denise Santoyo
Editorial Assistant:	Kathryn Journey
Cover Designer:	Michelle Lee

Contents

List of Tables and Figures   ix

Foreword   xiii
  Arthur L. Costa

Preface   xvii
  Acknowledgments   xviii

About the Authors   xxi

1. **Reflective Practice and Continuous Learning**   1
  What Is Reflective Practice and Where Did It Come From?   3
  What Is the Potential of Reflective Practice to Improve Schools?8
  What Does It Mean to Be a Reflective Educator?   9
  The Reflective Practice Spiral   11
    Individual Reflection   13
    Reflection With Partners   13
    Reflection in Small Groups and Teams   14
    Schoolwide Reflective Practice   15
    Moving Outward in the Reflective Spiral   17
  Closing   19

2. **Essential Questions**   22
  What Personal Capacities Promote Reflection?   23
    Promoting Trusting Relationships   23
    Expanding Thought and Inquiry   26
  What Makes Reflection Meaningful?   32

What Learning Principles Promote Reflective Practices? 37

What Learning Designs Promote Reflection? 39

Closing 41

3. Individual Reflection 43

Special Considerations for Reflecting on Our Own 45

Reflecting on Our Own: Examples From Practice 46

A 4-Step Reflection Process 46

Letting Your Reflections Flow 48

Reflection Directions 49

Five States of Mind 51

Reflecting on Our Own: More Ideas to Consider 52

Journaling 52

Mapping 53

Teacher Narratives 53

Teaching Portfolios 54

Metaphors 55

Reading With Reflection 56

Getting Started With Reflection on Your Own 56

4. Reflection With Partners 59

Special Considerations for Reflection Partners 61

What Is the Purpose of Your Partner Reflection? 61

With Whom Might You Reflect? 62

How Do You Reflect Together? 63

Reflection Partners: Examples From Practice 65

Reflective Voice Mail Bridges the Time Crunch 65

Reflective Practice in Paraprofessional Training and Teaming 66

Coaching: Three Examples 68

Schoolwide Dyads and Triads 70

Reflection Partners: More Ideas to Consider 71

Dialogue Journals 71

Structured Dialogue 71

Framing Experiences From Practice 72

Action Research 72

Weekly Reviews 73

	Listening Practice	73
	Observational Learning	74
	Getting Started With Reflection Partners	75
5.	**Reflection in Small Groups and Teams**	**78**
	Special Considerations for Reflection in Small Groups and Teams	80
	What Can Be Expected in Terms of Group Development Over Time?	81
	Who Participates and What Are Their Roles?	83
	What Structures and Processes Support Group Reflection and Learning?	91
	How Can Time Be Allocated for Learning Together?	99
	Reflection in Small Groups and Teams: Examples From Practice	100
	Time for Team-Learning Task Force	103
	Reading Reflection Groups in High School	106
	New Ways of Thinking About Space Allocation	107
	Reflection in Small Groups and Teams: More Ideas to Consider	110
	Metaphors	110
	Talking Cards	111
	Six Hats	112
	Think Tank	114
	Interactive Reflective Teaching	114
	Self-Organized Teacher-Support Groups	115
	Teacher Dialogues	115
	Video Clubs	116
	Teacher Book Clubs	116
	Reflection Roundtables	117
	Getting Started With Reflection in Small Groups and Teams	118
6.	**Schoolwide Reflection**	**121**
	Special Considerations for Schoolwide Reflection	123
	Creating Professional Learning Communities	124
	Facilitating Change at the Organizational Level	127
	Fostering Shared Leadership	129
	Schoolwide Reflection: Examples From Practice	133
	Reflecting Back to Reflect Forward at Mountain View School	133
	Inquiring Minds Unite at Urban High School	137
	Schoolwide Reflection: More Ideas to Consider	142
	Tapping the Community of Experts Within	142

Coaching Decreases Discipline Referrals	143
Learning in Faculty Meetings	143
Schoolwide Study Groups	144
Philosophy Club	145
Sharing School History	145
School Self-Review	146
Getting Started With Schoolwide Reflective Practice	147
Purpose . . . What and Why?	147
People . . . Who?	148
Design and Structure . . . How?	148
Outcomes . . . So What?	149
7. Moving Forward With Reflective Practice	**151**
Lessons Learned About Reflective Practice	152
Paradox of Reflective Practice	156
Closing	158
References	**161**

List of Tables and Figures

List of Tables

Table 1.1 Significant Contributions to the Thinking About
Reflective Practice   4

Table 2.1 Sampling of Topics to Promote Meaningful Reflection   34

Table 2.2 Questions to Prompt Different Levels of Reflection   36

Table 2.3 Conditions for Powerful Learning   38

Table 2.4 Sampling of Designs to Promote Staff Reflection and
Learning   40

Table 3.1 A 4-Step Process for Guiding Reflection   47

Table 4.1 Characteristics to Consider When Selecting a Reflective
Practice Partner   63

Table 5.1 Group-Member Roles   86

Table 5.2 Potential Advantages and Disadvantages of Internal and
External Facilitators   90

Table 5.3 Strategies and Examples of Time Allocated
for Staff Learning   101

List of Figures

Figure 1.1 A Comprehensive Definition of Reflective Practice   7

Figure 1.2 The Reflective Practice Spiral Illustrating Four Levels at Which Reflection Can Be Developed: Individual, Partner, Small Group or Team, and Schoolwide   12

Figure 1.3 A Web of Relationships Among Staff Members, Which Is Expanded and Strengthened Through Reflective Practice   18

Figure 1.4 Staff Resources for Student Learning That Are Enhanced Through Reflective Practice   20

Figure 1.5 Capturing Your Thoughts, Chapter Reflection Page   21

Figure 2.1 Illustrated Comparison Between the Processes of Dialogue and Discussion   31

Figure 2.2a Group Considering the Perspectives of Just Two Members   33

Figure 2.2b Group Considering the Perspectives of All Members   33

Figure 2.3 Capturing Your Thoughts, Chapter Reflection Page   42

Figure 3.1 The Reflective Practice Spiral With Individual Level of Reflection Highlighted   44

Figure 3.2 Reflection Directions   49

Figure 3.3 Sample Reflection Map on a Presentation About Classroom Management   54

Figure 3.4 Capturing Your Thoughts, Chapter Reflection Page   58

Figure 4.1 The Reflective Practice Spiral With Partner Level of Reflection Highlighted   60

Figure 4.2 Capturing Your Thoughts, Chapter Reflection Page   77

Figure 5.1 The Reflective Practice Spiral With Small-Group Level Highlighted   80

Figure 5.2 Diagram of Tuckman's (1965) Phases of Group Development   82

Figure 5.3 Reflective Practice Facilitator Position Description   89

Figure 5.4 Sioux Elder's Explanation of the Symbolism of Circles   94

Figure 5.5 Tabletop Norms   96

Figure 5.6 Sample of Closing Reflection Worksheets   98

Figure 5.7 Capturing Your Thoughts, Chapter Reflection Page   120

Figure 6.1 The Reflective Practice Spiral With Schoolwide Level of Reflection Highlighted   122

Figure 6.2 Emerging Framework for School-Based Professional Community   126

Figure 6.3 Adaptation of Ambrose's (1987) *Managing Complex Change* Model   128

Figure 6.4 Reflection Formats Used at Mountain View School   135

Figure 6.5 Sample Journaling Page   136

Figure 6.6 Supporting Structures and Desired Outcomes for the Inquiring Minds Initiative at Urban High School   139

Figure 6.7 Capturing Your Thoughts, Chapter Reflection Page   150

Figure 7.1 Reflection Mnemonic for Lessons Learned About Reflective Practice to Improve Schools   153

Figure 7.2 Paradox of Reflective Practice   157

Figure 7.3 Capturing Your Thoughts, Chapter Reflection Page   159

CORWIN
PRESS

The Corwin Press logo—a raven striding across an open book—represents the happy union of courage and learning. We are a professional-level publisher of books and journals for K–12 educators, and we are committed to creating and providing resources that embody these qualities. Corwin's motto is "Success for All Learners."

Foreword

Meaning making is not a spectator sport. It is an engagement of the mind that transforms the mind. The brain's capacity and desire to find patterns of meaning are keys of brain-based learning. Human beings are active, dynamic, self-organizing systems integrating the mind, body, and spirit. Their natural tendency is to organize experiences into greater levels of complexity and diversity. We never really understand something until we can create a model or metaphor derived from our unique personal world. The reality we perceive, feel, see, and hear is influenced by the constructivist processes of reflection. Humans don't get ideas, they make ideas.

Furthermore, meaning making is not just an individual operation. The individual interacts with others to construct shared knowledge. There is a cycle of internalization of what is socially constructed as shared meaning. Constructive learning, therefore, is viewed as a reciprocal process in that the individual influences the group, and the group influences the individual.

Children come fully equipped with an insatiable drive to explore, to experiment, and to inquire. Toddlers are in a constant state of exploring everything they can lay their hands, eyes, and lips on. They live in a state of continuous discovery: dismayed by anomaly, attracted to novelty, compelled to mastery, intrigued by mystery, curious about discrepancy. They derive personal and concrete feedback from their tactile and kinesthetic adventures. Their brains are actually being transformed with each new experience.

Unfortunately, the educational process often is oriented toward controlling rather than learning, rewarding individuals for performing for others rather than cultivating their natural curiosity and impulse to learn. From an early age, our fragmented curriculum teaches competitiveness and reactiveness. We are trained to believe that deep learning means knowing accepted truths rather than developing capacities for effective and thoughtful action; acquiring knowledge is for passing tests rather than accumulating wisdom and personal meaning. We are taught to value certainty rather than doubt, to give quick answers rather than to inquire, and to know which choice is correct rather than to reflect on alternatives. Learning is perceived to have little or no relevant application beyond the school to everyday living, further inquiry, or knowledge production.

Schools and classrooms today are busy, active places in which students and teachers are pressured with high-stakes testing to learn more, to learn faster, and to be held accountable for demonstrating to others their achievement of specified standards and mastery of content. For that reason, classrooms are much more present and future oriented than they are past oriented, and it is often easier to discard what has happened and simply move on. Thus children, whose natural tendency is to create personal meaning, are gradually habituated to think they are incapable of reflecting on and constructing meaning on their own. Eventually, students become convinced that knowledge is accumulated bits of information and that learning has little to do with their capacity for effective action, their sense of self, and how they exist in their world. Later, as they mature, they may confront learning opportunities with fear rather than mystery and wonder. They seem to feel better when they know rather than when they learn. They defend their biases, beliefs, and storehouses of knowledge rather than inviting the unknown, the creative, and the inspirational. Being certain and closed provides comfort whereas being doubtful and open causes fear. Life experiences and actions are viewed as separate, unrelated, and isolated events rather than as opportunities for continuous learning. Psychologists refer to this syndrome as an *episodic grasp of reality*.

Schools' and districts' improvement efforts may also signal an episodic approach. Proudly striving to keep abreast of educational improvement practices, some schools adopt an array of innovations (block scheduling, cross-grade groupings, multiple intelligences, interdisciplinary instruction, technology, mentoring, national standards, and so forth). Whereas a great deal of time may be spent in planning, limited time is spent in reflecting. As a result, teachers and administrators soon become impervious to integrating all the disparate pieces. In such an intellectually barren school climate, some teachers and administrators understandably grow depressed. Their vivid imagination, altruism, creativity, and intellectual prowess soon succumb to the humdrum, daily routines of unruly students, irrelevant curriculum, impersonal surroundings, and equally disillusioned coworkers. In such an environment, the likelihood that staff members would value reflectivity would be marginal.

The authors of this richly documented and valuable book provide a brighter vision. They believe that the organization that does not take time to reflect does not have time to improve and that reflective organizations view school improvement from a broader perspective, as a process of revealing and emancipating human and organizational resourcefulness. They make a strong case for the less-is-more principle and believe that to take the time, to set the tone, and to provide the opportunities for reflection prove beneficial not only for students but also for entire faculties. The time and effort invested in reflection yield a harvest of greater student learning, higher teacher morale, enhanced feelings of efficacy, and a more collaborative professional community.

They propose that a major but often overlooked goal of education should be habitual reflection on one's actions so as to maximize the autonomous, continual, and lifelong construction of meaning from those experiences. They offer compelling evidence that

- Reflecting on one's own work enhances meaning
- Constructing meaning from experiences enhances the applicability of that knowledge beyond the situation in which it was learned
- Insights and complex learning result from reflecting on one's experiences
- Reflecting on experiences is amplified when done with partners and in group settings
- Reflection by individuals is signaled and encouraged when reflection is implicit in the organization's values, policies, and practices

Maximizing meaning from life's experiences requires enhancing and amplifying the human capacities for reflection. To be reflective means to mentally wander through where you have been and try to make some sense out of it. Reflection involves such habits or dispositions as:

- Metacognition: Thinking about thinking and conducting an internal dialogue before, during, and after an event
- Connecting information to previous learning
- Drawing forth cognitive and emotional information from several sources: visual, auditory, kinesthetic, tactile
- Acting on and processing the information—synthesizing, evaluating
- Applying insights to contexts beyond the one in which they were learned

As individuals, staffs, and organizations reflect on their learning, they gain important information about how they perceive the efficacy of their planning, experimenting, data gathering, assessment, and self-modification. These experiences provide opportunities to practice the habit of continuous growth through reflection. The authors refer to this as the *reflective practice spiral*. Seizing opportunities to reflect individually, in partnerships, and in group situations within an atmosphere of trust, individuals, groups, and schools begin to learn how to become a continuously growing and learning professional community.

Reflection is not just kid stuff. The authors make a strong case for habitual reflection throughout the learning community—in students, teachers, administrators, and parents—as well as for integrating reflectivity in organizational practices. Because imitation is the most basic form of learning, impressionable students often need to see adults—parents, teachers, and administrators—reflect on their practice. Adults are not only facilitators of meaning making but also models of reflection. Their role is to help learners approach an event in a thoughtful and strategic way, to help monitor their progress during the experience, and to construct meaning from the content learned as well as from the process of learning it—and then to apply that learning to other contexts and settings. Educators in reflective schools and classrooms seek to ensure that all the inhabitants are fully engaged in the making of meaning, organizing experiences and activities so that stakeholders are the producers of knowledge rather than just the consumers of knowledge.

If the goal is to engage in deep reflection on one's work so as to make life experiences meaningful and to acquire the humility of continuous learning, then potent strategies must be employed in all quarters of the organization—for students, teachers, and administrators—and at all levels of the school community—in the classroom, in the school, in the school district, and in the community. Developing habits of continuous growth requires not only the capacity to be self-reflective; time also must be regularly scheduled to reflect on learning. Opportunities must be seized; strategies must be experimented with and evaluated for their productivity. And that is what this book so abundantly furnishes: clear directions for engaging in reflection individually, with partners, and in small and large groups; creative techniques for engaging in meaning making, clever ways to find the time, and practical strategies for deliberately setting an organizational tone of reflectivity.

We must vow to serve and maintain this natural tendency of humans to inquire and experience and, then, through reflection, find pattern, integrate meaning, and seek additional opportunities to satisfy the human propensity for learning. A goal of education, therefore, should be to recapture, sustain, and liberate the natural, self-organizing, learning tendencies inherent in all human beings: curiosity and wonderment, mystery and adventure, humor and playfulness, connection finding, inventiveness and creativity, continual inquiry, and insatiable learning through reflection.

The school that commits its resources of time, energy, and talent to reflection makes a clear statement of its valuing of the continuous intellectual growth for all its inhabitants and its desire to make the world a more thoughtful place.

—Arthur L. Costa, EdD
Kalaheo, Hawaii

Preface

Over the past decade, the language of reflective practice has started to permeate teacher-development and school-improvement research and practice. Given its apparent popularity, one might assume that nearly everyone must be doing it. In our work as educators, as facilitators of various school-improvement efforts, and as faculty members and advisors in graduate education, we have learned much about the potential and the challenges associated with embedding reflection as a norm in educational practice. The hectic pace and rigid structures in many of today's schools make it difficult to take time out to reflect and learn. The learning demands, however, continue to escalate for both students and staff.

Reflective practice is a vital resource for significant and sustained school improvement. Experience by itself is not enough. Reflection on experience is the pathway to improvement. Reflection is a means for examining beliefs, assumptions, and practices. It can lead to encouraging insights about instructional effectiveness. It can also result in the discovery of incongruities between espoused beliefs and actual actions. Either way, the self-awareness gained through reflection can motivate individuals to initiate changes in practice to enhance student learning. Effective implementation of reflective practice requires continuous development of both individual and organizational learning capacities.

The desired outcomes for readers of this book are (a) to understand the potential, if not the necessity, of reflective practice to improve teaching and learning in schools; (b) to initiate or extend individual commitments to reflective practice as a way to continuously learn and improve educational practice; and (c) to support implementation of individual and collaborative reflective practices within schools. Implied is the assumption that in order for students to learn well in school, so, too, must the community of educators around them. In the words of Art Costa (personal communication, April 1985), who wrote the foreword for this book and who is renowned for his work in cognitive coaching, "If we don't provide intellectually stimulating environments for teachers, why do we think they will provide that for students?"

This book offers a framework and strategies for thinking and acting as reflective educators. It is organized into seven chapters. In Chapter 1, we define reflective practice, provide a rationale for its potential to improve schools, describe char-

About the Authors

Jennifer York-Barr, PhD, is Associate Professor in the Department of Educational Policy and Administration at the University of Minnesota-Minneapolis. She received her PhD from the University of Wisconsin-Madison. Her work focuses on how educators work together to support student learning, particularly for students with various exceptionalities. She values highly the opportunities to continually learn with practicing K-12 colleagues through teaching, program development, and community-based research activities locally and throughout the United States and Canada. She coordinates graduate programs in teacher leadership, staff development, and educational administration and has received two distinguished teaching awards. She has authored over 100 publications, most of which are focused on collaboration and inclusive schooling.

William A. Sommers, PhD, is Assistant Professor of Education, Hamline University. He has been in K-12 education for 30 years as a teacher, assistant principal, and principal in urban, suburban, and rural schools, and has been an adjunct faculty member at the University of St. Thomas, St. Mary's University, the University of Minnesota, and Hamline University. He consults and trains in the areas of cognitive coaching, conflict management, organizational development, understanding poverty, group-dynamics facilitation, thinking skills, and brain research.

As part of his doctoral program, his dissertation researched teaching and modeling reflective models and how this affected students in the classroom. With a minor in industrial relations, he reads books and articles constantly in the area of business management and leadership in addition to educational literature. He sees that solutions in the future for our complex problems will be a combination of education and business. Learning is his main personal goal, but he worries about the continual separation of the haves and have-nots. Learning is about freedom.

Gail S. Ghere, MA, is a project coordinator for a federal grant that focuses on instructional team collaboration for students with disabilities in inclusive schools. She has her MA in special education and is a doctoral candidate in program evaluation in the Department of Educational Policy and Administration at the University of Minnesota. For almost 25 years, she has worked in rural, suburban, and urban public schools as a related service provider supporting students with disabilities. Over this period, her belief in creating inclusive opportunities for students with disabilities has continually led her to be involved in collaborative projects. In her ongoing work with both general and special educators, reflection is routinely embedded into the learning opportunities.

Jo Montie has her MA in Educational Psychology from the University of Minnesota and works to foster the development of inclusive communities of compassion, collaboration, and inquiry. She is also a community volunteer and change agent. The children and adults in her life provide ongoing lessons about the need to be surrounded by a web of loving relationships, the importance of contribution and social change, and the capacity for reflection that exists in all of us. Previous professional work includes serving as a special education teacher, school consultant and staff-development facilitator, and project coordinator with the University of Minnesota's Institute on Community Integration.

1

Reflective Practice and Continuous Learning

The ultimate guardians of excellence are not external
forces, but internal professional responsibilities.

—Paul Ramsden (1992, p. 221)
Learning to Teach in Higher Education

Learning is the foundation of individual and organizational improvement (Argyris, 1977; Argyris & Schon, 1974). Learning requires reflection. From an individual perspective, "It can be argued that reflective practice . . . is the process which underlies all forms of high professional competence" (Bright, 1996, p. 166). From an organizational perspective, reflective practice is considered a powerful norm in schools in order to achieve high levels of student learning (Hawley & Valli, 2000; Kruse, Louis, & Bryk, 1995). It is becoming increasingly clear that when educators engage in high-quality learning experiences, the impact on student learning is positive. Reflective practices facilitate learning, renewal, and growth throughout the development of career educators (Steffy, Wolfe, Pasch, & Enz, 2000). Sparks-Langer and Colton (1991) explain the recent emphasis on reflective practice in schools:

> The shift toward an interest in reflective thinking has come about partly as a reaction to the overly technical and simplistic view of teaching that dominated the 1980s. Gradually, however, experts in supervision, staff development, and teacher education have begun to recognize that teaching is a complex, situation-specific dilemma ridden endeavor. . . . Today, profes-

sional knowledge is seen as coming both from sources outside the teacher and from the teachers' own interpretations of everyday experience. (p. 37)

Most educators experience a continuously hectic pace in their daily professional lives. Such a pace is not conducive to reflection and learning. The dominant culture in many schools is one of doing, with little or no time for reflection and learning. The context of teaching has been referred to as *hot action*, meaning that "educators must develop habits and routines in order to cope; and [that] self-awareness is difficult as there is little opportunity to notice or think about what one is doing" (Eraut, 1985, p. 128). It is not unusual for teachers to put aside carefully constructed lessons due to unanticipated circumstances or responses. It is also not unusual for those same lessons to become fragmented as a result of the constant coming to and going from classrooms by students and staff. Educators routinely must juggle multiple tasks, process information on many levels, and make on-the-spot decisions to meet the changing needs and demands in the teaching environment. On some days, the intensity of teachers' work might be aptly compared with that of air traffic controllers. Glickman (1988) describes an inherent dilemma for the teaching profession as having "knowledge but not certainty" (p. 63). Within each specific teaching context lie multiple and unpredictable circumstances that require spontaneous and unique responses. The demand for accountability and the steady flow of curricular and instructional initiatives add to the challenging context of teaching. The critical balance between pressure and support for improvement (Fullan & Stiegelbauer, 1991) is almost always on tilt toward the side of pressure. Shifting from a culture of doing to a culture of learning while doing is not easily accomplished.

Given these challenging context variables, why is it reasonable to assume that significant improvements in educational practice are possible? What changes in the culture of schools are necessary to support continuous learning and development of educators? Where does an individual educator start? One of the purposes of this book is to support practicing educators in the development of capacities within themselves and within their schools to continuously learn and improve by embedding the norm of reflective practice in their work. A major premise is captured by the Chinese proverb, "Sometimes you must go slow to go fast." Reflective practice cannot be done in the fast lane. Although much of educational practice occurs in the fast lane, educators must find or create a rest area along the roadside to reflect on past practices and to determine appropriate adjustments for future practice.

In this chapter, multiple perspectives on the meaning of reflective practice are shared. A rationale for the potential of reflective practice to improve schools is articulated. The characteristics of reflective educators are described. Presented last is the reflective practice spiral, which serves as the organizing framework for the book. This framework suggests that the seeds of reflective practice begin first within individuals and then spread into the broader educational community.

What Is Reflective Practice and Where Did It Come From?

Reflective practice is as much a state of mind as it is a set of activities.

(Vaughan, 1990, p. ix)

A review of the origins of reflective practice and its evolution to the present day indicates a substantial history and base of knowledge. The thinking about reflection and reflective practice has evolved over a period of many decades if not centuries, through carefully constructed theory, research, and application. Numerous theorists, researchers, and teacher educators have contributed to this body of knowledge. John Dewey is frequently recognized as the foundational 20th-century influence on reflection in education (Hatton & Smith, 1995; Sparks-Langer & Colton, 1991; Zeichner & Liston, 1996). His work, however, drew from much earlier Eastern and Western philosophers and educators including Buddha, Plato, and Lao Tzu. In more recent years, the work of Donald Schon (1983, 1987) has inspired a resurgence of interest in reflective practice in the field of education.

Some of the significant contributions to the thinking about reflective practice are highlighted in Table 1.1. Each of the authors' conceptions add to or extend a significant consideration in our understanding of reflection and reflective practice. Collectively, the literature on reflective practice reveals numerous common themes. Reflection is viewed as an active thought process aimed at understanding and subsequent improvement. Both personal and contextual variables influence the reflective process and outcomes. Reflection can occur in different ways and for different purposes. Reflection that considers social, moral, and ethical perspectives has the potential to affect community values and action.

What is reflective practice? Reflective practice is an inquiry approach to teaching that involves a personal commitment to continuous learning and improvement. A commitment to reflective practice indicates a willingness to accept responsibility for one's professional practice (Ross, 1990). Reflection is not "the mindless following of unexamined practices or principles" (Sparks-Langer & Colton, 1991, p. 37). It is not the "pointless reflection of one's navel as symbolized by Rodin's 'The Thinker' " (Bright, 1996, p. 166). It is not just getting together to talk about work or thinking self-reinforcing thoughts about how to teach.

There is no universally accepted definition of what reflective practice is, but numerous perspectives are offered in the literature, each of which has a slightly different emphasis. Listed here are perspectives that have been offered by different authors. Reflective practice can be considered

- "The practice or act of analyzing our actions, decisions, or products by focusing on our process of achieving them" (Killion & Todnem, 1991, p. 15)

TABLE 1.1 Significant Contributions to the Thinking About Reflective Practice

---

Dewey, 1938

- Considered the goal of education to be the development of reflective, creative, responsible thought (Hatton & Smith, 1995)
- Was interested in how people think when faced with real and relevant problems
- Viewed learning as an ongoing interaction between the individual and context

---

Van Manen, 1977

- Suggested three levels of reflectivity to describe various aims of reflection: *technical reflection*, which focuses on examining the skills, strategies, and methods used to reach predetermined goals (e.g., Is this the most effective way to accomplish this goal?); *practical reflection*, which focuses on examining the methods used to reach goals and also reexamining the goals themselves (e.g., Is this a worthy goal to strive for?); and *critical reflection*, which focuses on inquiring about the moral, ethical, and social equity aspects of practice (e.g., Does this promote equity, and for whom?)

Zeichner, 1987, 1993

- Argued the essential role of critical reflection in education, emphasizing that educators must critically examine how instructional and other school practices contribute to social equity and to the establishment of a just and human society
- Challenged the assumption that education will necessarily be better if teachers reflect, because reflection can validate and justify current practices that are harmful to students

---

Schon, 1983, 1987

- Described a "crisis in professional knowledge," referring to the gap between professional knowledge and actual competencies required for practicing teachers
- Used the terms *the swamp* to connote the ambiguity, uncertainty, complexity, and oftentimes conflicting values that define the daily teaching context, and *swamp knowledge* to describe the tacit knowledge teachers develop from construction and reconstruction of their swamp experiences
- Differentiated between *reflection-in-action*, referring to the process of observing our thinking and action as they are occurring, in order to make adjustments in the moment, and *reflection-on-action*, referring to the process of looking back on, and learning from, experience or action in order to affect future action (Note: Killion and Todnem (1991) expanded Schon's reflection-in-action and reflection-on-action typology to include reflection-for-action)

TABLE 1.1 Continued

Smyth, 1989

- Suggested four forms of action that can guide reflection on practice: *describe* (e.g., What do I do?), *inform* (e.g., What does this mean?), *confront* (e.g., How did I come to think or act like this?), and *reconstruct* (e.g., How might I do things differently?)

Osterman and Kottkamp, 1993

- Emphasized the influence of underlying, personal-action theories on behavior
- Brought attention to consideration of the theories or views that individuals talk about (i.e., espoused theories) versus the theories or views that are evident in watching individuals behave (i.e., theories in use), suggesting reflective practices as a way to examine and uncover underlying theories and views that affect action

---

Sparks-Langer and Colton, 1993; Langer and Colton, 1994

- Identified multiple influences on the knowledge construction involved in reflective practice: experiential knowledge, professional knowledge, feelings, the surrounding collegial environment, and personal characteristics or attributes
- Introduced a cyclical process, referred to as the Framework for Developing Teacher Reflection, that includes these steps: Gather information about an experience or event; conduct analysis by considering multiple influencing variables; form hypotheses; and then test hypotheses through implementation

---

Butler, 1996

- Argued that professional development must be self-directed and that reflection is the central process for integrating knowledge and experience
- Expressed concern that externally prescribed training disempowers the problem-solving process of educators, thereby creating dependence on "the system" instead of promoting the internal capacities of practicing professionals

---

- "The capacity of a teacher to think creatively, imaginatively and in time, self-critically about classroom practice" (Lasley, 1992, p. 24)
- "Deliberate thinking about action with a view to its improvement" (Hatton & Smith, 1995, p. 40)
- "A genuinely critical, questioning orientation and a deep commitment to the discovery and analysis of positive and negative information concerning

the quality and status of a professional's designed action" (Bright, 1996, p. 165)

- "An active, proactive, reactive and action-based process" (Bright, 1996, p. 167)

- "A way of thinking about educational matters that involves the ability to make rational choices and to assume responsibility for these choices" (Ross, 1989, p. 22)

- "An active and deliberative cognitive process, involving sequences of interconnected ideas which take into account underlying beliefs and knowledge" (Dewey, as described in Hatton & Smith, 1995, p. 34)

Drawing on the perspectives offered above and on our own work, we identify the following as elements of a comprehensive definition: Reflective practice is a deliberate pause to assume an open perspective, to allow for higher-level thinking processes. Practitioners use these processes for examining beliefs, goals, and practices, to gain new or deeper understandings that lead to actions that improve learning for students (see Figure 1.1). Actions may involve changes in behavior, skills, attitudes, or perspectives within an individual, partner, small group, or school. Each of these elements is described briefly here.

Reflective practice requires a *deliberate pause*, a purposeful slowing down of life to find time for reflection. To deliberately pause creates the psychological space and attention in which an open perspective can be held. Kahn (1992) emphasizes the importance of psychological presence as a requisite for individual learning and high-quality performance. In between a stimulus and a response is a moment of choice (Covey, 1989)—a pause during which options for actions can be considered. Human beings have the capacity to choose their responses to life's experiences (Frankl, 1959). When reflecting, people choose deliberately to pause as a precursor to considering appropriate responses.

An *open perspective* or open-mindedness (Dewey, 1933; Ross, 1990; Zeichner & Liston, 1996) means being open to other points of view. It means recognizing that represented within a group are many ways to view particular circumstances or events. It means being open to changing viewpoints and letting go of needing to be right or wanting to win (Webb, 1995). Rather, the purpose is to understand. Openness to other perspectives requires a mindful and flexible orientation. Mindful people are awake (Nhat Hanh, 1993) and conscious of thought and actions. Being awake includes having an awareness of others and extending learning beyond the immediate sphere. In education, awareness extends from immediate instructional circumstances to caring about democratic foundations and encouraging socially responsible actions (Sparks-Langer & Colton, 1993). Doubt, perplexity, and tentativeness are part of openness (Dewey, 1933; Langer & Colton, 1994). An open perspective creates the possibility for the emergence of new understandings and increasingly more effective responses.

Reflection involves active and conscious *processing of thoughts*. Thinking processes, such as inquiry, metacognition, analysis, integration, and synthesis, may all

Figure 1.1. A Comprehensive Definition of Reflective Practice

be used in a reflective process. Reflection, for example, may take the form of self-observation and analysis of one's own behaviors and the perceived consequences. It may involve group members' being aware of their thoughts during a decision-making process for determining differentiated instructional objectives and strategies (Hatton & Smith, 1995). Higher-level thinking processes provide the means to move beyond a focus on isolated facts, events, or data to perceive a broader context for understanding.

The focus of reflection involves *examination of beliefs, goals, and practices.* Beliefs include people's values, visions, biases, and paradigms. Beliefs stem largely from one's experiences and significantly influence ways of thinking and behaving. Beliefs create the lens through which we view our worlds. Goals encompass desired aims, outcomes, or intentions. They can be very general or specific in nature. General goals may address such desires as creating a learning community for students. Specific goals may address more concrete and immediate aims, such as teaching children how to learn effectively in groups during social studies. *Practice* refers to one's repertoire of dispositions, behaviors, and skills in specific areas of performance, such as designing instruction and assessment strategies, interacting with students, developing relationships with families, collaborating with colleagues, and implementing schoolwide reforms.

A desirable outgrowth of reflection is new or *deeper understanding and insights.* Such understanding provides the basis for considering new forms of action. Awareness and understanding are critical elements for initiating and sustaining change in practice. New understandings without changes in behavior, however, will not make differences in the lives of students. Application of knowledge is essential (Dewey, 1933; Smyth, 1989). Reflective practice leads to improvement only when deepened *understandings lead to action.*

Reflective practice provides a way "to understand and make sense of the world" (Brubacher, Case, & Reagan, 1994, p. 36). It is an active process. "Rather than reflective practice being seen as impractical, passive, or irrelevant to action, it can be regarded as centrally important and relevant to the understanding of ongoing action" (Bright, 1996, p. 167). It serves as the foundation for continuous learning and improvement in educational practice so that children are successful in school and in life. It is a complex process that requires high levels of conscious thought as well as a commitment to making changes based on new understandings of how to practice. Reflective practice must not be viewed as yet another bandwagon—here today, gone tomorrow. It has the potential to significantly improve education if its foundations and assumptions are honored. Unless the integrity of reflective practice is upheld, efforts at implementation will be superficial and will result in few positive gains.

What Is the Potential of Reflective Practice to Improve Schools?

Increasing evidence suggests what common sense has always told us: Student learning is linked with staff learning. This means that as staff members learn and improve their instructional practice, students benefit and show increases in learning (Richardson, 1997, 1998).

> The main objective of reflective practice is to ensure a more accurate and relevant understanding of a situation such that professionally designed action in that situation is more likely to produce effective, relevant action which will facilitate the occurrence of more desired and effective outcomes. (Bright, 1996, p. 177)

In education, the desired outcomes are increases in student learning and capacity to learn, with learning broadly conceptualized as including academic, social, and emotional well-being. High levels of student learning require high levels of staff competence. Reflective practice increases the potential of schools to improve for at least the following reasons:

- It creates the *opportunity to continuously learn* from and about educational practice. If educators do not reflect on and learn from their practice, they are likely to continue doing what they have been doing. Recall the old adage, "If you always do what you've always done, you'll always get what you've always gotten."

- Practitioners have a *greater variety of perspectives* to draw on in addressing the many challenging and complex dilemmas of practice. Consideration of different perspectives can result in more effective solutions, which are more broadly understood, accepted, and implemented.

- *New knowledge and understandings* that have immediate applications to practice are created. Knowledge constructed within the context of practice is needed to effectively teach the increasing variety of school-age children and youth. By sharing newly constructed knowledge among colleagues, the impact for improvement can be multiplied.

- *Efficacy* increases as educators see the positive effects on their own context-generated solutions. Efficacy refers to the belief that one can make a difference in the lives of students. As the internal capacities of teachers are recognized and tapped, a greater sense of empowerment emerges.

- Professional educators themselves assume *personal responsibility for learning* and improvement. Rather than relying on the system for training programs to substantially improve or fix the instructional process, educators come to rely on themselves and one another.

- *Strengthened relationships and connections* among staff members emerge. As continuous improvement becomes a shared goal and reflection becomes embedded in practice, isolation is reduced, and relationships strengthen, giving rise to a foundation for schoolwide improvement.

- Educators can build *bridges between theory and practice*. They consider externally generated knowledge from the research community and then determine appropriate, customized applications or combinations of applications to their specific context of practice.

- *A reduction in external mandates* may ultimately result when educators are viewed as effectively addressing many of the challenges of practice. The belief that externally prescribed interventions must be mandated if schools are to improve could be challenged.

What Does It Mean to Be a Reflective Educator?

What do reflective educators look like? How do they behave? How would you know a reflective educator if you met one? One of the distinguishing characteristics of reflective educators is a high level of commitment to their own professional development (Zeichner & Liston, 1996). They have a sustained interest in learning. Inquiry, questioning, and discovery are norms embedded in their ways of thinking and practice (Bright, 1996; Zeichner & Liston, 1996). Their inquiry focuses not only on the effectiveness of their instruction but also on the underlying assumptions, biases, and values that they bring to the educational process. They consider issues of justice, equity, and morality as they design and reflect on their practice. Their interest in learning is continually sparked by triggers of curiosity about some aspect of practice (Clarke, 1995). Instead of blindly accepting or rejecting new information or ideas, they carefully examine, analyze, and reframe them in terms of specific context variables, previous experiences, and alignments with desired educational goals (Clarke, 1995; Costa & Garmston, 1988; Zeichner & Liston, 1996). Reflective educators are decision makers who develop thoughtful plans to move new understandings into action so that meaningful improvements result for students (Clarke, 1995; Costa & Garmston, 1988).

As described previously, the work of educators takes place in a dynamic, unpredictable, and sometimes ambiguous context. Reflective educators recognize that much of the knowledge about effective practice is tacit, meaning that it is learned from experience within the practice context. To learn in and from that context, reflective educators are keenly aware of their surrounding context, are open to and seek feedback, and can effectively distill the information that should be considered in a reflective process (Bright, 1996). We offer the profile of a reflective educator as one who

- Is committed to continuous improvement in practice
- Assumes responsibility for his or her own learning
- Demonstrates awareness of self, others, and the surrounding context
- Develops the thinking skills for effective inquiry
- Takes action that aligns with new understandings

Distinctions are appropriately made between reflective educators, also referred to as reflective practitioners, and experts, in terms of how knowledge is viewed and generated (Schon, 1987; Webb, 1995). Generally speaking, two major sources of knowledge to bring to bear on practice are externally generated knowledge and internally created knowledge. Externally generated knowledge comes by way of the research community and usually offers generalized findings, directions, and strategies for consideration by the practicing community. This is sometimes referred to as technical-rational or content knowledge. Internally created knowledge comes by way of reflecting on practice and customizing use of externally generated knowledge to unique contexts of practice, that is, specific schools, classes, and students. This is sometimes referred to as contextual knowledge.

Reflective practitioners draw largely from an experiential or contextual knowledge base in which "it is impossible to disentangle knowing from doing" (Webb, 1995, p. 71). Content experts draw largely from a technical-rational knowledge base (Schon, 1983). They are masters of content but may not have the practice background that generates tacit knowledge about how to apply, use, or teach content in the classroom. Webb (1995) explains that from the technical-rational knowledge perspective of content experts,

> Professional practice rests upon an underlying discipline or basic science producing general theory and knowledge which the professional practitioner then applies to individual daily problems . . . [in] professional practice . . . knowing directs doing, and those who know are the experts. (p. 71)

This perspective explains some of the disconnect that educators sense when learning from experts of content who cannot make the application to the classroom context. It also speaks to the frustration or cynicism that can arise among practicing educators when content experts assume an easy transfer of technical-rational knowledge to the context of practice.

For some aspects of practice, educators draw on a technical-rational knowledge base, such as disciplinary expertise. For example, math teachers draw on the technical knowledge base of the discipline of mathematics. For many other aspects of daily practice, though, educators draw on their experientially and contextually derived knowledge from practice. Schon (1983) explains that when, as reflective practitioners,

> We go about the spontaneous, intuitive performance of the actions of every day life, we show ourselves to be knowledgeable in a special way. Often we cannot say what it is we know. When we try to describe it, we find ourselves at a loss, or we produce descriptions that are obviously inappropriate. Our knowledge is ordinarily tacit, implicit in our patterns of action and in our feel for the stuff with which we are dealing. It seems right to say that our knowing is in our action. (p. 9)

Both types of knowledge—content and context—are necessary to achieve excellence in practice. It is the job of the educators to adopt a reflective stance, to continually expand their understanding and repertoire of practice. In doing so they realize both the challenges and benefits of lifelong learning: "Significant learning generally involves fluctuating episodes of anxiety-producing self-scrutiny and energy-inducing leaps forward in ability and understanding" (Brookfield, 1992, p. 12). Such is the journey of a reflective educator.

The Reflective Practice Spiral

The reflective practice spiral (Figure 1.2) presents one way to think about initiating and expanding efforts to embed reflective practices as a cultural norm in schools. It

Figure 1.2. The Reflective Practice Spiral Illustrating Four Levels at Which Reflection Can Be Developed: Individual, Partner, Small Group or Team, and Schoolwide

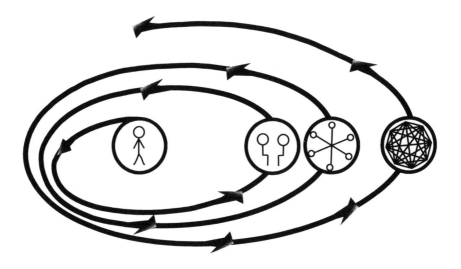

reflects an assumption that the place to begin is with oneself. The reflective practice spiral has four levels: individual, partner, small group or team, and school wide. The spiral that moves through the levels represents the interconnectedness among the levels, resulting in a cumulative effect on schoolwide practices. The innermost circle that illustrates just one person represents the individual level of the spiral. The partner level is represented in the second circle showing two individuals interacting. The small-group level is represented in the third circle, shown as six individuals connected around a common purpose in the center. The outermost circle in the spiral symbolizes schoolwide involvement as represented by a web of connections among people, which extends throughout the school.

Lived experience is perhaps the most powerful influence on the formation of beliefs and values, which are the driving forces behind actions. The positive growth that individuals experience from reflective practice provides a more solid foundation for advocacy and for the sustained commitment required to expand the practice of reflection beyond themselves. As we develop our individual reflection capacities, we can better influence the reflection that occurs with partners and in small groups or teams of which we are members. As more groups become reflective in their work, the influence of reflection begins to spread throughout the school. A critical mass of individuals who have experienced positive outcomes from their own reflective practice and from reflection within groups and teams can better support widespread adoption.

Each level in the reflective practice spiral is described below, along with the potential benefits at each level. Examples and specific considerations for implementation at each level are addressed in Chapters 3 through 6.

Individual Reflection

This is the level at which each of us, as an educator, has full responsibility and control and can choose to use reflective practices in our work and life. Reflection on our own provides each of us with the opportunity to realize the following gains:

- Improvements in educational practice, given greater awareness of personal performance, increased recognition of dilemmas that arise in practice, different ways of thinking about dilemmas, and resulting adjustments in practice

- Increased student learning and learning capacities, given improvements in personal practice

- Increased personal capacities for learning and improvement, as the skills and dispositions for reflective practice become embedded in our way of thinking and doing

- Restored balance and perspective, given the time-out created for reflection and the subsequent learning; learning is a great source of inspiration!

- Renewed clarity of personal and professional purpose, given a sense of empowerment to align our practice with purpose

Some ways to reflect alone include journaling, reviewing a case, reading professional literature, developing and reviewing a teaching portfolio, exercising, and observing or listening to one's own practice through use of videotapes or audiotapes. Chapter 3 contains additional considerations and specific examples of individual reflective practice. When beginning to learn more about reflective practice and its potential, through individual experience, we are in a position to more effectively assist others in creating and supporting the development of reflective capacities in others. In doing so, our own reflection and learning are also enriched.

Reflection With Partners

Joining with another person in the process of reflection can result in greater insight about one's practice, especially when trust is high, and the right combination of support and challenge is present. Partner reflection can also introduce an element of fun. Humor, when appropriately interjected, can remind us not to take ourselves too seriously and to remember that mistakes are an inevitable part of the ongoing learning and improvement process. In addition to the gains that can be realized at the individual level of reflection, adding a partner to the reflection process can result in

- Expanded learning and confidence about our own practice, given the different perspective of another person and the assistance of coaching, a process of inquiry

- Increased professional and social support and decreased feelings of isolation at work, given the presence of a strengthened collegial relationship

- An increased sense of who we are and how things work in our school, given the connection and exchange with another person who also experiences life in our place of work

- Greater commitment to work and the work environment, given our increased feelings of confidence and connection to another person in the place of work

Some ways that two people can reflect together include interactive journaling, cognitive coaching, conversing about instructional design possibilities, talking through steps of an inquiry cycle related to specific events or dilemmas, reading and talking about articles or case studies, examining student work, and even reflecting with a partner online. Chapter 5 contains additional considerations and specific examples of reflective practice for partners. The increased sense of competence, support, and connection that can emerge from reflection with a partner positions us on more solid ground to extend the practice of reflection to small groups.

Reflection in Small Groups and Teams

There is a big shift from reflecting alone or with a partner to reflecting in a small group, such as a team or committee. While the potential impact of reflection increases, so does personal risk. Because more people are in a group, the sense of safety and connection between individuals is not the same as in partner reflection. Groups and teams are also frequently appointed or mandated, whereas partner reflection is usually more voluntary and self-organized. In appointed or mandated groups, there is frequently less control over two important factors: the individuals who are present and the commitment and desire to participate. Composition and commitment affect interactions and outcomes.

Despite the risks involved in expanding reflective practice to such groups, good reasons exist to venture forth into this domain. When reflection becomes part of educational practice within a small group, its members can realize the following gains:

- Enhanced learning and resources for learning about practice, given the expanded number of individuals—each of whom brings varied experiences and expertise in life, learning, and education

- Increased professional and social support, given the expanded network of collegial relationships

- More effective interventions for individual students or groups of identified students, given shared purpose, responsibility, and expertise among members of a group

- Emerging sense of hope and encouragement that meaningful and sustained improvements in practice can occur, given that members in a group are working and learning together

- Improved climate and collegiality, given greater understanding of our own and others' experiences and perspectives about our shared place of work

Some ways to reflect in a small group include action research, study groups, regular grade-level or content-area meetings to review and design instructional and assessment procedures, and case-study reviews. Reflective practices can also enhance committee work by intentionally engaging in reflection about past practices and future possibilities and by soliciting the perspectives of people representing broad interests in the respective work. Arguably, committees that form to address building-wide concerns such as space, scheduling, extracurricular activities, and remedial supports for learning would be more effective if reflection and learning were an embedded part of the committee process. Within groups, it is often appropriate to include a participatory reflection process that focuses on how the group is working together and accomplishing its objectives. Refer to Chapter 5 for more considerations and specific examples of reflective practice in groups or teams.

At the small-group level of reflective practice, the potential to influence more broadly the educational practices begins to emerge within and throughout the school. Small ripples of change frequently become the impetus for much broader changes, even when that was not an original intent (Garmston & Wellman, 1995; Wheatley, 1992). The potential to improve educational practices significantly increases when multiple groups and teams succeed in embedding reflective practices in their work, and when efforts expand to include the vast majority of individuals and groups in a school.

Schoolwide Reflective Practice

The greatest potential for reflective practice to improve schools lies with the collective understanding, thinking, learning, and acting that result from schoolwide engagement. Over the past decade, emphasis on schoolwide, as opposed to isolated, improvement efforts has increased (e.g., Calhoun, 1994). Isolated efforts (e.g., initiatives taken on by individual teachers, grade levels, or content areas) typically result in only isolated improvements, with few cumulative gains realized once students move on from those experiences. Furthermore, effects do not spread to other groups of students without intentional efforts to design and implement new practices with those students. These are some of the reasons for the emergence of practices intended to promote professional community, focused on increasing student learning (Fullan, 2000a; Hord, 1997; King & Newmann, 2000; Louis & Kruse, 1995; Newmann & Wehlage, 1995). When reflection becomes part of educational practice on a schoolwide basis, the following gains can be realized:

- Greatly expanded learning opportunities, resources, and the potential to achieve schoolwide improvements in educational practice

- Enhanced communication about students among teachers within and across grade levels and curricular areas

- Increased professional and social support through the expanded network of relationships and understanding of others' experiences at work

- Increased sense of shared purpose and responsibility to all students

- Increased understanding of how the school works and how schoolwide improvement efforts might be successful

- Increased sense of possibility for meaningful and sustained improvements in practice, given expanded awareness of the commitments and talents of a broad network of people in the school

Reflective practices at the schoolwide level can take many forms. An entire school staff may be involved in study groups on a common topic, such as reading in content areas or performance assessment. There might also be groups or teams across the school with varied purposes. For example, interdisciplinary groups could form to share disciplinary expertise and to create a set of integrated student outcomes that would be addressed within each of the content areas or to evaluate the design and effectiveness of a specific initiative. Cross-grade-level teams might explore the best practices for effective student transitions between grades or schools. Some issues require schoolwide attention and participation, so group composition should be intentionally designed to connect people across grade levels or curricular areas to bring forth different perspectives. This also results in relationships forming between individuals who may not typically cross paths during a school day. It is neither possible nor necessary to include every staff member in every learning or shared-work initiative. What matters most is that staff members are involved in some type of learning or shared-work initiative, in addition to being committed to their continued professional development and improvement. Chapter 6 contains additional considerations and specific examples of reflective practice at the school level.

Moving Outward in the Reflective Practice Spiral

As reflective practice grows from the center of the reflective practice spiral, moving from the individual toward the schoolwide level, there is greater potential to affect schoolwide change. The potential at the outer levels is based on the assumption that individuals continue to enhance their own reflection and learning. Resources, information, perspectives, ownership, commitment, relationships, and shared leadership increase substantially because greater numbers of staff members are involved and learning together.

As reflective practice spirals out from the center, challenges to effective implementation are greater. Complexity is dramatically increased due to the greater numbers of people involved. Interpersonal dynamics become a greater force. Logistics, such as scheduling time for reflection, become more difficult. Individual risk is greater because an individual's perspectives are exposed to a greater number of people with whom there may be varying degrees of trust, respect, and commitment. The surrounding context and climate of a school also have a greater effect as practices expand to include more people. There are long-standing structures that reinforce isolation. The history and established cultures within and across groups create invisible barriers to interaction. Multiple and often competing priorities for time and professional development can fragment focus, effort, and people. In addition, lack of support from formal and informal leaders in the building undermines efforts to move forward. In short, as the individual moves out in the spiral, there is more potential but also more complexity and less control.

Recognizing the presence of significant, complicating variables at the school level can raise serious doubts about the feasibility of reflective practice. It is easy to become overwhelmed by the inherently complex nature of schoolwide change. This is one of the reasons that the reflective practice spiral is proposed as a guiding framework. We can choose to remain committed to our own professional learning and improvement by embedding reflective practices in their lives. We can at least engage in reflective practices at the individual level. Choosing to assume a responsible, proactive stance toward our own development adds positive energy to our lives and to the environments in which we work. As individuals, we reap the benefits of continuous learning, and we increase our professional competence. Learning also renews our spirit. Our human needs to learn and grow can be met, in part, through reflective practices. A commitment to the individual level of reflective practice is beneficial for us as individuals and also has an indirect effect on others.

Beyond the individual, then, the potential for improvement in schools increases with each additional person who chooses to make a commitment to professional learning and improvement. Recent understandings about how organizations or systems evolve suggest that significant changes arise through the relationships and interactions among people (Garmston & Wellman, 1995; Wheatley, 1992). Also suggested is that change happens in ways we cannot predict or control. As each of us continues to learn, and as we reach out to connect and learn with others,

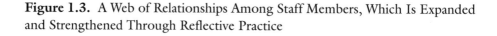

Figure 1.3. A Web of Relationships Among Staff Members, Which Is Expanded and Strengthened Through Reflective Practice

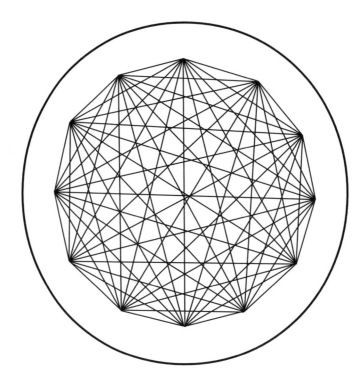

relationships form and strengthen, thereby increasing the potential for improvement on a larger scale.

Combinations of different groups of staff members learning together throughout the school result in expanded and strengthened relationships among all staff members. In effect, a *web of relationships* forms to facilitate communication and connection throughout the school community (Figure 1.3). This web of relationships serves several very important functions: (a) A safety net is created for students, who are less likely to feel anonymous and fragmented because staff members are in better communication about students, especially those who are struggling in school; (b) a rich network of resources—people and information—is formed, and any member of the school community can tap it; if someone in our immediate network does not know something, we are likely to be connected to someone in another network who may know; and (c) when we are more tightly coupled with others in our work, there is a greater likelihood of more comprehensive, effective, and rapid response to schoolwide issues, ranging from safety concerns to adoption of new curricula. To enhance the web metaphor for school improvement, consider that the threads of weaver spiders are one of the strongest organic materials that nature produces. In laboratories, scientists harvest the threads and weave them into bullet-proof vests. Thus the web is an apt metaphor for the durable and protective community that emerges and spreads from the spinning of many individuals.

To envision how the web of relationships can accomplish these important functions, look at Figure 1.3 and think of it as representing a well-connected and effective community of educators in a school. Now picture something falling onto the web. The specific something could be a student with unique challenges, a new program or curriculum, or new teachers. Because of all the interconnections, whatever falls onto the strands of the web is caught. The web flexes to accommodate its presence, so it does not fall to the ground underneath. Every connection (relationship) in the web knows that something new has arrived and can offer resources and support. Without these connections, whatever lands in the school (web) falls to the ground and is on its own to establish the connections needed to survive. A web of relationships can embrace a new presence, connect it to the broader community, and bring forth resources needed to effectively interact with or respond to the new presence in the web. Reflective practice is one significant means of forming and strengthening the relationships, which are the verbal, social, behavioral, and emotional connections that constitute the web.

Closing

Education is about learning—not only student learning but also staff learning. Learning is a function of reflection. "Adults do not learn from experience, they learn from processing experience" (Arin-Krupp as cited in Garmston & Wellman, 1997, p. 1). Dewey asserted years ago that experience itself is not enough. Ten years of teaching can be 10 years of learning from experience with continuous improvement, or it can be 1 year with no learning repeated 10 times. Learning and improvement can no longer be optional. Reflection, therefore, must be at the center of individual and organizational improvement initiatives.

Reflective practice offers one powerful way for educators—individually and collectively—to stay challenged, effective, and alive in their work. The greater the number of people involved, the greater the potential to significantly improve educational practice and, therefore, the greater the potential to enhance student learning. Figure 1.4 identifies staff resources that emerge when educators in a school join together to reflect and learn, with a commitment to continuous improvement. Despite the hectic pace and the steady demands, increasing numbers of educators are making it a priority to create space in their professional lives for reflection and learning. In doing so, they are being nurtured to grow and are expanding their repertoire of effective instructional practices. They are moving from a culture of doing to a culture of learning.

Figure 1.4. Staff Resources for Student Learning That Are Enhanced Through Reflective Practice

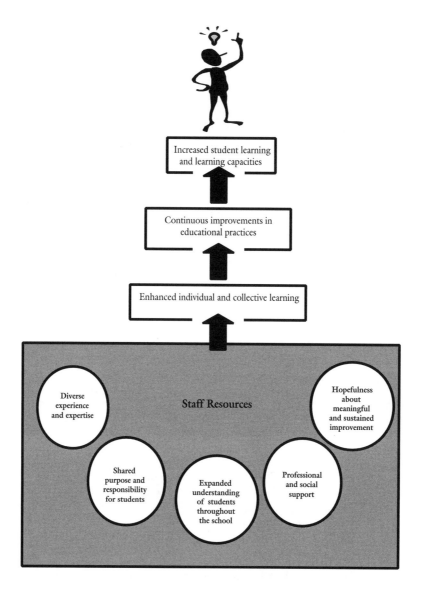

You are invited to use the Chapter Reflection: Capturing Your Thoughts form (Figure 1.5) to make note of significant learning or insights sparked from reading Chapter 1. In the next chapter, the focus shifts away from the foundational elements of reflective practice to focus on strategies and tools to promote reflection. Specifically, personal capacities that promote reflection will be described along with other essential elements to consider in the design and implementation of reflective practices to improve schools.

Figure 1.5. Chapter Reflection: Capturing Your Thoughts

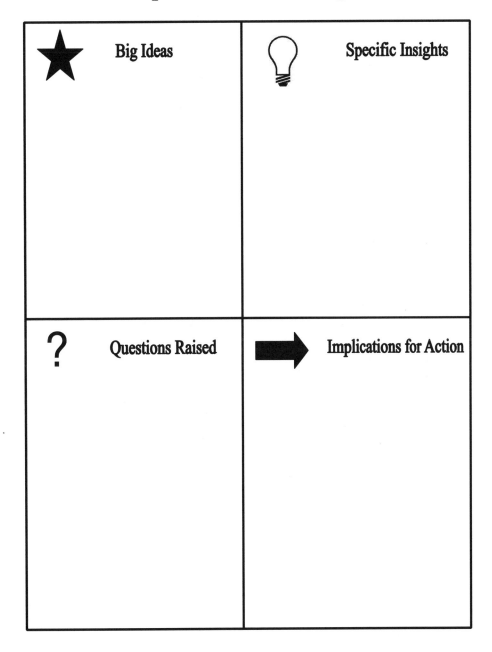

2

Essential Questions

We learn by conversing with ourselves, with
others, and with the world around us.
—Sheila Harri-Augstein & Laurie Thomas
(1991, p. 3)
Learning Conversations

The purpose of reflective practice is to increase learning at the individual and organizational levels (Kim, 1993) so that educational practice continuously improves and student learning is enhanced. Specific goals of reflective practice are

- To review a process to see if it achieved the desired goals or outcomes
- To make learning visible
- To complete the learning cycle for each incident in our lives
- To give a more considered response to an event
- To achieve meaning and understanding inside actions
- To add value to self and to performance
- To move us from novice to expert (Butler, 1996, pp. 271-272)

Harri-Augstein and Thomas (1991) propose that educators accomplish such goals by engaging in a learning conversation, which they describe as a means of increasing awareness about our own learning processes and of challenging our conditioned ways of thinking, being, and doing. With these goals in mind, the questions become How do we have conversations about learning? and What are the essential elements that promote reflection and learning together?

The purpose of this chapter is to describe essential elements of reflective practice at all levels of the reflective practice spiral—individual, with partners, in small groups, and schoolwide. To do this, we address four questions:

- What *personal capacities* promote reflective practices?
- What *topics* promote reflective practices?
- What *learning principles* promote reflective practices?
- What *learning designs* promote reflective practices?

Following this chapter, in Chapters 3 through 6, we offer specific examples of how these essential elements are addressed in a variety of contexts to address specific goals.

What Personal Capacities Promote Reflection?

Personal capacities for reflection refer to the skills and dispositions that enhance one's ability to reflect on and learn from practice. Individual educators can choose to develop these capacities on their own, regardless of whether or not colleagues also choose to do so. It is more difficult to develop personal capacities for reflection if the surrounding environment is not supportive, but it is possible. In this section, we identify personal capacities focused on two essential conditions for reflective practice: *trusting relationships* and *thought and inquiry*.

Promoting Trusting Relationships

The quality of relationships is a key determinant of the quality of reflection and the potential for learning (Ellinor & Gerard, 1998; Wheatley, 1992). Relationships influence the emotion with which one approaches reflection, and emotion controls the gateway to learning (Wolfe, 1997). Most specifically, trust must be present for individuals to share their thoughts and to be open to expanding their ways of thinking and doing.

> Trust is perhaps the essential condition needed to foster reflective practice in any environment. If the reflective process is going to flourish in an orga-nizational setting, the participants must be confident that the information they disclose will not be used against them—in subtle or not so subtle ways. (Osterman & Kottkamp, 1993, p. 45)

Recent research offers supporting evidence that trust is an important requisite for reflection and learning together. For example, a study of professional commu-nity in 248 elementary schools found that "by far, the strongest facilitator of pro-fessional community is social trust among faculty members. When teachers trust and respect each other, a powerful social resource is available for supporting the collaboration, reflective dialogue, and deprivatization characteristics of professional community" (Bryk, Camburn, & Louis, 1999, p. 767). Without trust, there is no foundation for a relationship focused on learning. Learning requires change. Change involves risk. "No one will talk about problems—personal or organizational—unless they feel safe, secure, and able to take risks" (Osterman & Kottkamp, 1993, p. 45). Stated more emphatically, Tom Peters, renowned author and business consultant, is reported to have said, "The degree to which one takes risks is inversely proportional to the potential for being shot."

To be in a trusting relationship with oneself or others requires acting in trustworthy ways. These interrelated skills and dispositions that promote trustworthiness are described below: Be present, be open, listen without judgment and with empathy, seek understanding, view learning as mutual, honor the person, and honor the process. The choice to behave in these ways can be difficult, given the pervasive norms of fast paced doing in many schools. Developing and integrating these skills and dispositions into our daily lives requires explicit, ongoing attention.

Be present. Being present with oneself and others is an acknowledgement of value. It involves being aware of oneself, others, and the surrounding environment. "To be aware is to allow our attention to broaden and expand to include more and more of our immediate experience. The central idea here is that we are capable of coming to understand what is happening as it is happening" (Isaacs, 1999, p. 144). To be fully present and aware is a conscious choice and requires putting aside competing priorities. It creates the psychological space to be open to one's own and others' thoughts.

Kahn (1992) describes how individuals who are psychologically present can bring themselves more fully to their work and to interactions with others at work, resulting in higher levels of productivity. He explains that

> The long term implication of such presence is that people who are present and authentic in their roles help to create shared understandings of their systems that are equally authentic and responsive to change and growth. This process is what allows social systems . . . to become unstuck and move toward new and productive ways of working. When individuals are open to change and connecting to work with others and are focused and attentive and complete rather than fragmented, their systems adopt the same characteristics, collectively. Individual and systemic wholeness, in these respects, are intertwined and complementary. (p. 331)

Be open. Being open is a state of mind in which multiple perspectives can be considered. It requires hearing different views as valid ways of thinking, not as threats. "Openmindedness is an active desire to listen to more sides than one, to give full attention to alternative possibilities, and to recognize the possibility of error even in beliefs that are dearest to us" (Zeichner & Liston, 1996, p. 10). Exposure to different viewpoints is critical in fostering inquiry by providing additional information, which may contrast with current views (Diss, Buckley, & Pfau, 1992; Hatton & Smith, 1995; Levin, 1995). In the absence of openness, reflection merely validates and perpetuates one's own current views. At the core of being open is a belief that there are multiple, valid ways of experiencing, making sense of, and acting in the world.

Listen without judgment and with empathy. Closely related to being open is the ability to listen well, without judgment and with empathy. Listening and learning are closely linked. If we do not listen well, we do not learn well. Our tendency is to listen from memory, screening and interpreting what is being said through our own filter of experiences, values, and beliefs (Carlson & Bailey, 1997; Isaacs, 1999). When we listen this way, a speaker's intended meaning may be lost or misinterpreted. Listening well requires an awareness and suspension of our own thoughts so the focus is on the speaker's experience and intended meaning (Garmston & Wellman, 1999; Lee, 1995). "To suspend is to change direction, to stop, step back, and see things with new eyes. This is perhaps one of the deepest challenges humans face—especially once they have staked out a position" (Isaacs, 1999, p. 135). This explains, in part, why it is so difficult to listen well. The listeners' own ways of thinking or acting are at risk of being changed or influenced (Rogers, 1986).

Empathetic listening involves an even deeper sense of genuine connection with another person, a feeling of strong connection not only to the words but also to the emotion felt and expressed by that person. "Empathic relationships generally confer the greatest opportunity for personal, and thus professional, growth in educational settings" (Rogers as described by Butler, 1996, p. 265). Listening is perhaps the greatest gift we can offer one another, and in the process, we can foster the growth of a reflective community of educators.

Seek understanding. Understanding is an outgrowth of listening well. To understand other people's thoughts and actions is to make sense of their core identities. To do so in a nonjudgmental way is to validate their humanness. Understanding, but not necessarily agreeing, is one of the strongest and most respectful ways of connecting with another person (Covey, 1989). When educators feel understood by their peers, they can more easily let go of needing to be right and holding onto their views. They can also more easily let go of judgments and negative assumptions. Mutual understanding promotes trust, which, as emphasized earlier, is the foundation for reflective practice.

View learning as mutual. To view learning as mutual means that all partners in a reflection process are learners and derive benefit. Schools are hierarchically structured organizations with unequal value assigned to individuals depending on age, years of experience, degrees held, and even grade level or content area taught. Too often, younger and less experienced teachers who do not hold graduate degrees are socialized into thinking they are of less value in their school community. Of course, the reverse can also be true when more experienced teachers are stereotyped as lacking an interest in continued growth and change. Even when experience varies greatly between individuals, there should be an earnest valuing of the potential to learn from and with others. This stance rejects the presence of experts and assumes value in the perspective of each individual. Many mentors, for example, comment that their experience of mentoring teachers who are relatively new to the profession has enriched their learning and understanding about practice. Educators committed to reflective practice should "approach all situations [and people] with the attitude that they can learn something new" (Zeichner & Liston, 1996, p. 11).

Honor the person. Perhaps the greatest threat to reflection and learning is to in some way dishonor a person. Talking behind someone's back, sharing information that was offered in confidence, or building coalitions that exclude are acts of dishonoring people and commitments to learning and working together. Reflective educators should choose always to honor people by offering the same degree of respect that they wish to be shown.

Honor the process. Process has developed a bad reputation in some circles. Granted, engaging in too much process without meaningful outcome is not time well spent. Developing capacities for reflective practice, however, takes time, explicit attention, practice, and feedback. There is no fast lane to creating a reflective learning community. Trusting relationships develop over time through multiple interactions in which individuals demonstrate trustworthy behaviors toward their colleagues. Thinking capacities, especially collective thinking capacities, also develop over time as individuals learn how to reflect and think together. Recall the learning curve presented in introductory psychology courses. At first, engaging in new ways of thinking and doing feels awkward, inefficient, and even ineffective. There is a tendency to disengage early in the learning process. Over time, however, new ways of thinking and doing become more fluid, automatic, and embedded into daily life. Do not give up on the process too soon. The benefits of reflective practice come slowly to fruition. Also pay attention to others, assisting those who become discouraged or impatient. Stay the course and recall again the Chinese proverb, "Sometimes you must go slow to go fast."

Expanding Thought and Inquiry

From a foundation of trusting relationships, expanded ways of thinking and genuine inquiry can emerge. "It is only through the process of inquiry that awareness, understanding, and competence are developed and realized" (Bright, 1996, p. 177). In this section, we describe three interrelated sets of strategies for expanding thinking capacities: asking questions, responding with SPACE, and engaging in dialogue.

Ask Open Questions

At the heart of reflective practice is inquiry. Inquiry is an active search for understanding, which is facilitated by carefully constructed questions. Perkins (1992) in his book *Smart Schools* said, "Learning is a consequence of thinking" (p. 8). Our corollary is that thinking is a consequence of questions (Sommers, 1995). A powerful question alters all thinking and behaving that occurs afterward (Goldberg, 1998). Statements tend to spark analytic thinking and judgment. Questions, on the other hand, tend to spark creative thinking and generate either a search for answers, a negotiation of meaning, or a continuation of dialogue. Inquiry is the seed of ongoing reflection, which helps people to construct their own meanings and become partners in helping others to construct the same.

Because language constructs everyone's reality, the language chosen when asking questions has a major impact on emotion, the learning environment, and ultimately personal identity as a learner. *Intonation, syntax,* and *presuppositions* have been identified as key linguistic elements in posing effective questions (Costa & Garmston, 1988). Each is described briefly here.

The nonverbal quality of *intonation* sends a message of intent. Intonation refers to how the message sounds. Intonation tends to be a more accurate discriminating variable than the content of a question. When asking questions, speakers need to align intonation with inquiry. Grinder (1993) identifies two kinds of voice intonation. One is referred to as *credible voice,* the other as *approachable voice.* Credible voice is used when giving directions or making statements that need to be viewed as credible or directive. The voice has a flat intonation pattern and drops at the end. Approachable voice is used when asking questions or wanting input. This voice has an intonation pattern that fluctuates up and down, and it ends with voice going up. An approachable voice communicates genuine inquiry and should be used when posing questions intended to prompt reflection.

A second element of asking questions is *syntax,* or how the question is structured. The nature of responses provided depends on the nature of the questions asked. If questions ask for recall, answers tend to be short and to the point. There is no elaboration. If the syntax of questions suggests making comparisons, contrasting different events, analyzing, or some other means of active processing of thoughts, answers are longer, with greater breadth and depth. If the syntax is structured to engage consideration of positive potential, such as, "What might be the best possible results when doing this presentation?" or "If you taught the perfect lesson, how would it look?", people start to construct a positive future. When the mind is actively involved in constructing responses, the likelihood of behaving in congruent ways is increased. If people cannot internally or verbally construct positive outcomes, they encounter difficulty in moving forward to accomplish their desired goals.

A third element of asking questions to promote reflection and metacognition is *presupposition.* Presuppositions are very powerful. They work whether they are negative or positive. The reason they are powerful is that groups act as if presuppositions are true. For instance, when one of the authors was a newly hired principal at a high school, a staff member told him, "It's too bad that 250 of these students won't be here in the spring." The principal was shocked by this statement (a presupposition), but in the spring, 250 students had dropped out. If people believe that some kids can't learn, they will be correct. Reportedly, Henry Ford once said, "Whether you think you can or think you can't, you are right." Presuppositions that are stated positively can facilitate achieving more positive results. Embedding positive presuppositions in the structure of language can assist reflection on previous actions (reflection back) as well as reflection for future action (reflection forward).

Most of the time, educators are either planning a future event or reflecting back on something they already did. Following are examples of questions that may be helpful in promoting reflective thinking in these circumstances. As you read the questions, consider how intonation (e.g., credible voice), syntax, positive presuppositions, and use of an approachable voice might affect responses.

- As you think about the last time you taught this lesson, what are some of the outcomes you want to have happen again?

- When you reflect back on your lesson, what would you do differently next time you teach this lesson?

- As you think about the results you got, what were some of the ways you designed the lesson to cause them to happen?

- When you think about what you had planned and what actually happened, what were the similarities and what were the differences?

- How do you think the lesson went? What happened that caused it to go that way?

- What are some of the professional goals that you are working on for yourself?

- Who or what are the resources for you as you work toward your professional goals?

Respond With SPACE

The way in which a person responds to another person influences thinking and inquiry just as much as questioning does. Costa and Kallick (2000a) present SPACE as an acronym for response strategies that prompt reflection: silence, paraphrase, accept nonjudgmentally, clarify, and extend.

If the intent of responding is to promote reflective thinking, time must be provided to think. Sometimes, this requires *silence* on the part of the listener. There is an Estonian Proverb that says, "Silence is sometimes the answer." In our very harried lives, we tend to want answers quickly. But for reflection to occur, less is frequently more. One clue for determining whether partners are processing is to watch their eyes. When someone is thinking, the eyes are usually up or moving. When done thinking, the eyes come back to center and refocus on others. If people are interrupted with more questions or information while in the midst of thinking, they never have a chance to complete their thoughts. Silence allows people to think.

Paraphrasing requires listening. When listeners paraphrase, the speakers know that they have been heard. Paraphrasing is not *parrot phrasing*. In other words, listeners should not say exactly the same thing the speakers just said. Such responses can be interpreted as mocking restatements or as lacking sincere interest. Paraphrasing is taking the main concepts or ideas and saying them back as if you are trying to understand. Some sentence stems to use are:

- Let me see if I understand; you said . . .
- I want to make sure I got all the points; you said . . .
- You said [this], and then you said [this], and then . . . Is that right?

Paraphrasing communicates trying to understand. If listeners have the wrong information, it can be corrected through further restatement.

Accepting nonjudgmentally is the third response strategy in the SPACE acronym. If listeners want a stream of meaning to come forth, accepting what people are saying will initiate more thought processes. Interrupting with the listeners' own viewpoints or responding with apparent disagreement will inhibit the process. Judgment shuts down thinking whether it is praise or rejection (Deci, 1995; Kohn, 1993).

Clarifying is the next responding behavior that can increase reflection and metacognition. If a teacher says, "I want the students to know the causes of the Vietnam war," a facilitator might respond, "What will the students be doing or saying that will give you that information?" By asking clarifying questions, teachers can clarify in their own minds the desired student responses. This kind of reflection happens only when people take the time to ask naive questions that internally illuminate the meaning. When asking clarifying questions, be sure to use proper intonation (i.e., approachable voice) so clarifying does not sound like interrogating or accusing.

Extending is the last response strategy of the SPACE acronym and one that is easily and frequently used. The following sentence stems, for example, call for an extension of people's thinking:

- Say more about . . .
- Tell me more about . . .
- Some other possible connections are . . .

Using these stems gives a chance for people to extend their thinking beyond what they have already considered and discussed. Although breakthroughs are not created at every use, they do create an opportunity for additional consideration of the subject.

Another strategy for extending thinking is to ask *take-away questions*. For instance, "As we end our conversation, what are the possible connections to the team goals?" Take-away questions frequently cause continued thought and reflection. It is not unusual for people to show up the next day and say, "I have been thinking about our conversation and . . ." This is a sign that people are participating fully in the reflective process.

Engage in Dialogue

The power of dialogue to promote reflection and learning has been emphasized by many authors (Bohm, 1996; Ellinor & Gerard, 1998; Garmston & Wellman, 1997, 1999; Isaacs, 1999; Vella, 1994). Dialogue has been described as a "conversation with a center, not sides" (Isaacs, 1999, p. 19) and as a "living experience of inquiry within and between people" (Isaacs, 1999, p. 9). It is a process of verbally sharing and also thinking together for the purposes of expanding thinking, promoting understanding, making connections, and generating possibilities. It is an open process in terms of structure and outcome. "Thinking together implies that you no longer take your own position as final. You relax your grip on certainty and listen to the possibilities that simply result from being in relationship with others—possibilities that might not otherwise have occurred" (Isaacs, 1999, p. 19). Dialogue can also be a way to get unstuck by uncovering underlying assumptions and beliefs that are blocking effective thinking and action (Ellinor & Gerard, 1998).

Dialogue is frequently contrasted with discussion (Ellinor & Gerard 1998; Garmston & Wellman, 1997, 1999; Isaacs, 1999). As depicted in Figure 2.1, dialogue can be thought of as an opening-up process in which participants discover new perspectives and connections and arrive at fresh understandings, insights, and connections. Discussion can be thought of as a narrowing, eliminating, or closing-down process. The purpose of dialogue is to increase understanding; the purpose of discussion is to make decisions. Both processes are necessary ways of conversing, but the important distinction needs to be made about when each is most appropriate. Moving to discussion and decision making before adequate dialogue often leads to decisions that lack sufficient information and to decisions that do not stay made. Underlying the thinking about dialogue is a theory that shared meaning leads to shared thinking, which leads to aligned action.

Some decisions are not important enough to warrant a group going through an extensive, participatory process of dialogue before decision making. For example, the color of copying paper or the location of the pop machine usually would not be worthy of extended periods of conversation. But important and complex decisions that affect many students and staff members benefit from consideration

Figure 2.1. Illustrated Comparison Between the Processes of Dialogue and Discussion

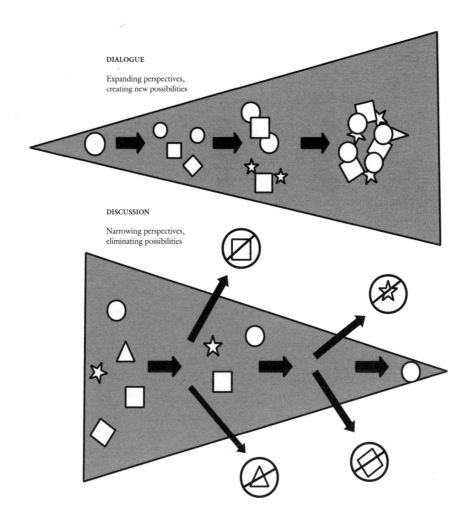

of many diverse perspectives: for example, how should new students and families be welcomed to school, or how can our schedule be developed to allow coteaching between general and special educators during language arts? For these types of decisions, all the resources in a group should be tapped for at least two reasons. First, decisions should be made on the richest set of information. Second, participation in perspective sharing and decision making increases the likelihood that decisions will stay made and will be implemented. People can usually live with decisions when they feel their viewpoint has been understood and when they understand the basis for a decision.

For an illustration of the difference in outcomes when using an inclusive dialogue (instead of a focused discussion) prior to making a decision, refer to the diagram of two groups in Figure 2.2a and Figure 2.2b. Each diagram shows a group of 12 people, indicated by the circled letters, seated in a circle. In the top circle, only person A and person H share their respective perspectives with the rest of the group (represented by the letters A and H in the center of the circle). In the bottom circle, each of the 12 individuals share their respective perspectives with the group (represented by all the letters in the center of the circle). Now, consider that each group makes a decision about how to proceed based on the perspectives shared (i.e., the perspectives in the center of each circle).

- Which group had more people actively participating?
- Which group probably learned the most during its conversation?
- Which group had a richer set of perspectives from which to base a decision?
- Which group might have discovered several new possibilities for moving forward?
- Which group's members are more likely to honor and abide by whatever decision is made?

This exercise visually illustrates two different ways that groups can converse and the likely consequences of each type of conversation. The group in the bottom circle could be thought of as having engaged in a dialogue. The group in the top circle is more likely to have moved quickly to discussion and thereby limited the number of perspectives shared.

Unfortunately, in schools, many conversations about important topics look like that of the top group in Figure 2.2. Only a few perspectives are shared, resulting in poorer-quality decisions and in decisions that are not honored by all group members. Not surprisingly, therefore, some topics appear repeatedly on group agendas. Ironically, we don't think we have the time to engage in dialogue before moving to decisions, yet we end up allocating time to address the same issues over and over and over again. Perhaps more up-front time would lessen the amount of time spent down the road. A proactive stance that creates space for dialogue about important issues may ultimately be more effective and efficient.

What Makes Reflection Meaningful?

> *Adults learn, retain, and use what they perceive*
> *is relevant to their professional needs.*
> (McGregor et al., 1998, p.4)

It cannot be overstated that the focus of reflection should be relevant to practice. Knowledge, techniques, and processes that improve educators' effectiveness

Figure 2.2a. Group Considering the Perspectives of Just Two Members

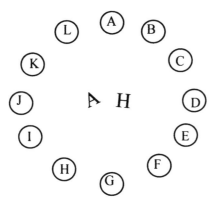

Figure 2.2b. Group Considering the Perspectives of All Members

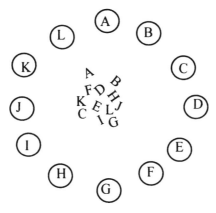

with students are powerful motivators for learning. The primary rewards of teachers are known to lie in the accomplishments of students (Lieberman & Miller, 1999; Rosenholtz, 1989). Without a meaningful focus, efforts to establish reflective practices in school will not be successful. What constitutes meaningful? There are at least four major influences: topic or content, depth or level of application, opportunity to strengthen relationships, and opportunity to learn. Each of these factors is discussed briefly below.

Topic refers to the content focus of reflection. A specific topic or focus may be precipitated by feelings such as dissonance, dismay, frustration, surprise, curiosity, and conflict (Clarke, 1995). This supports the assertion that improving personal practice serves as a motivation for professional learning. Some authors assert that learning for professionals should be largely self-directed (Bailey, Curtis, & Nunan,

TABLE 2.1 Sampling of Topics to Promote Meaningful Reflection

Focus on students

- Understanding individual student strengths, challenges, learning styles, and interests
- Observing or listening to students work to determine problem-solving, organizational, and learning strategies
- Reviewing student work to determine overall levels of performance and specific interventions
- Analyzing patterns of social interaction and effectiveness among students
- Determining effective student groupings to support learning, participation, access, and equity
- Reviewing curricular materials to determine appropriateness, given student abilities, interests, and background as well as broader community values

Focus on self

- Understanding of conceptual underpinnings of curricular emphases and how all the parts fit together to create a meaningful whole
- Determining the effectiveness of various instructional strategies for specific content areas and context factors
- Paying attention to individual as well as group learning needs and strengths
- Examining personal biases or conflicts with students, peers, or parents
- Revisiting personal purpose, values, and beliefs and their alignment with teaching designs and behaviors
- Being inclusive and supportive of colleagues
- Assuming responsibility for team and schoolwide initiatives

Focus on staff

- Determining assignments for instructional teams focused on specific groups of students
- Developing supportive mentoring and induction experiences for staff members who are new to the building
- Intentionally including colleagues in reflection and learning efforts

Focus on school

- Creating the schoolwide schedule to embed collaborative learning opportunities for teams of teachers
- Examining space to determine appropriate use, given instructional needs of students

TABLE 2.1 Continued

- Designing effective communication systems to connect and keep informed all members of the school community
- Setting priorities for educational improvement initiatives
- Focusing site-based governance practices on issues of increased student learning

Focus on community

- Extending meaningful opportunities for parent and community involvement
- Soliciting input and support for school goals
- Seeking participation by community resource personnel
- Sharing information and improvements with the surrounding community

1998; Butler, 1996) because identified topics will be of specific interest to the individuals involved.

To improve student outcomes, the overarching focus of reflective practices must be somehow related to student learning (Bryk et al., 1999; Newmann & Wehlage, 1995). Within this broad domain, more specific emphases are targeted depending on specific context and student needs (e.g., early literacy, interdisciplinary instruction in middle schools, authentic assessment in algebra, community-work experience, or collaborative services for students with mild disabilities). Table 2.1 presents an illustrative sampling of topics that might be meaningful emphases for reflection. (Throughout Chapters 3 to 6, specific examples illustrate how meaningful topics surfaced as essential features of successful reflective practices.)

Depth or level of reflection refers to the specific aim of reflection within a given topical focus. Three levels of reflection have been described in the literature: technical, practical, and critical (Grimmet, MacKinnon, Erickson, & Riecken, 1990; Hatton & Smith, 1995; Taggart & Wilson, 1998; Van Manen, 1977). A *technical focus* of reflection examines methods or technique; a *practical focus* examines both goals and methods of practice; and a *critical focus* examines not only goals and methods but also outcomes from a moral, ethical, and social perspective. With this latter focus, "reflection is an intellectually active, critical, and extending process by which teachers appreciate the implications of their classroom decisions in terms of the immediate needs of students and the broader goals of society" (Lasley, 1992, p. 26). Table 2.2 offers examples of questions that guide reflection at these levels.

There is evidence that early-career teachers and expert teachers reflect differently and at different levels. Expert teachers have a much richer set of experiences (tacit knowledge) to draw on as resources than do novice teachers. In a classic study, Berliner (1986) found that

TABLE 2.2 Questions to Prompt Different Levels of Reflection

Stage 1 reflection: a technical focus

- What practices are and are not effective in the classroom?
- What problems require attention?
- What approaches can be used by the teacher to correct problem situations?
- Is the class organized and well managed?

Stage 2 reflection: a conceptual focus

- What is the espoused philosophical or theoretical basis for current practice?
- Are the teacher's classroom practices consistent with the teacher's espoused philosophy?
- Does current practice appear to foster or diminish student attentiveness to assigned tasks and learning?

Stage 3 reflection: a dialectical focus

- Is the philosophy of the teacher consistent with the needs of the students?
- What teacher practices enhance or diminish student growth?
- What student needs are not addressed by current teacher and school practices?
- How should schools be reordered and restructured?
- And what must teachers do to facilitate such restructuring?

SOURCE: Adapted with permission from Lasley, T. J. (1992). Promoting teacher reflection. *Journal of Staff Development, 13*(1), 24-29. May not be reproduced without permission.

> Experts possess a special kind of knowledge about learners that is different from that of novices . . . and of a very different order than is subject matter knowledge . . . it is knowledge that influences classroom management and is the basis for transferring subject matter. (p. 10)

It has been suggested that richly developed schemata of expert teachers, as related to student differences and to contextual variables, result in designing more effective learning environments and solving problems at a much higher level than novice educators (Sparks-Langer & Colton, 1991). Experts are also able to see problems from a broader context and are able to draw on their tacit knowledge to determine effective interventions and supports.

Early-career teachers tend to focus their attention at the more technical level of reflection (Ross, 1990; Sparks-Langer, Simmons, Pasch, Colton, & Starko, 1990). Leat (1995) explains that early-career teachers need to focus primarily on the immediate classroom context, including classroom management and relationships with students. He found that too much emphasis on reflection at higher levels could be the source of considerable stress. Reflection at higher and deeper levels tends to occur more frequently in experienced teachers. Regardless of the level of reflection or the career stage of an individual teacher, reflection is viewed as the process by which teachers continue to improve their practice and move from novice to expert (Butler, 1996; Steffy, Wolfe, Pasch, & Enz, 2000).

The final two influences on making reflective practices meaningful are closely related: *opportunities to strengthen relationships* and *opportunities to learn*. The opportunity to learn with colleagues is of high interest to many educators. It can satisfy needs to be in association with others and to continue learning. For example, members in study groups who were focused on the topic of literacy reported that their primary interest in participating was the opportunity to learn with and get to know other educators (Henry et al., 1999).

Ultimately, the determination of meaningfulness is individually constructed. For some educators, topical focus will be the largest determining factor. For others, the opportunity to learn with colleagues may, at least initially, prove more influential. For many, a combination is important.

What Learning Principles Promote Reflective Practices?

Adult learning is voluntary in all its dimensions—
participation, acquisition, and outcome.

(Even, 1987, p. 22)

There is an extensive research base about the conditions that foster learning in adults. When considering how to implement reflective practices in schools, what is known about adult learners and learning should guide the design process. When adults enter any learning situation, they immediately begin to filter information based on the depth of their knowledge about the topic as well as on the whole repertoire of their life experiences. They employ ongoing problem-solving and questioning processes that require attending to new material and ways of thinking, structuring the information to understand it at a deeper level, integrating new knowledge with previous learning, and finally, working the new knowledge into greater degrees of application, abstraction, and generalization. The learning process is not linear. Adult learners continually cycle back and forth between current knowledge and new knowledge, employing the problem-solving and inquiry process (Even, 1987).

Merriam (1993), a renowned scholar in the area of adult learning, articulates fundamental values about adult learning from which principles for facilitating reflective practices can be derived:

TABLE 2.3 Conditions for Powerful Learning

In general, we can say that people learn well under the following conditions:

What they learn

1. What they learn is personally meaningful.
2. What they learn is challenging, and they accept the challenge.
3. What they learn is appropriate for their developmental level.

How they learn

4. They can learn in their own way, have choices, and feel in control.
5. They use what they already know as they construct new knowledge.
6. They have opportunities for social interaction.
7. They get helpful feedback.
8. They acquire and use strategies.

Where they learn

9. They experience a positive emotional climate.
10. The environment supports the intended learning.

SOURCE: Reprinted by permission from Brandt, R. (1998). *Powerful Learning*. Alexandria, VA: Association for Supervision and Curriculum Development. May not be reproduced without permission.

- The individual is at the center of education.
- There is goodness in each individual, and there is a need to release and trust that goodness.
- Learning should result in growth toward one's potential.
- Autonomy and self-direction are signposts of adulthood.
- There is potency in the individual to achieve self-direction and fulfillment in the face of social, political, cultural, and historical forces. (p. 133)

Brandt (1998) draws from numerous sources (e.g., American Psychological Association, 1997; Caine & Caine, 1997) to summarize conditions that promote what he refers to as "powerful learning" (see Table 2.3). He emphasizes that the content of learning must be meaningful and relevant to learners, the process of learning must allow opportunities to reflect on past experiences and is also enhanced by social interaction, and the context of learning must be supportive emotionally and structurally.

Taken together, the works of Even (1987), Merriam (1993), and Brandt (1998) point to several implications for the design of reflective practices for educators. First, educators must be respected as self-directed learners and recognized as in charge of their own learning. Second, reflective practices must be grounded in the educator's context of practice. Third, opportunities should be provided to examine underlying beliefs, values, and assumptions in order to achieve deeper understanding of teaching and learning processes. Fourth, when introducing new information or perspectives, the reflective learning process must allow opportunities to compare and contrast, link, and integrate old and new perspectives. In sum, significant learning for educators involves an active process of knowledge construction drawing from experience, making sense of new ways of thinking, and moving toward application in the context of practice.

What Learning Designs Promote Reflection?

Reflection can occur alone or with others, and depending on the purpose and on specific context variables, there are many ways to design or structure reflective practices. Structures refer to how the reflective learning process is organized. Who is involved? How many people are involved? Is the reflection process casual and free-flowing or prescribed and facilitated? What information serves as the focus of reflection? How are the outcomes of reflection incorporated into practice? Reflection can be fostered by journaling after teaching, analyzing videotapes of teaching, engaging action research, observing others teach and engaging in dialogue after the observations, assessing student performance, conversing with colleagues or with students about student learning, examining case studies, shifting from a problem-solving to a problem-framing perspective, and actively linking theory and practice (Clarke, 1995; Sparks-Langer & Colton, 1991).

Teachers seem to use different types of learning designs or structures depending on the focus of the learning objective (Parades-Scribner, 1999). For example, to learn about instructional strategies and classroom management, teachers viewed collaborating with peers as most beneficial. To learn more about a content or discipline area, individual inquiry and access to outside expertise (e.g., information delivered in workshops) was viewed as most helpful. To learn more about social factors influencing students and the school, teachers relied most on their own experience.

The summer issue ("Powerful Designs of Learning" 1999) of the *Journal of Staff Development* (JSD) presents a comprehensive menu of designs to promote staff learning. Each learning design is described, examples are provided, and additional resources are identified. A sampling of the learning designs introduced in the issue is briefly summarized in Table 2.4. When determining which specific learning designs are most appropriate for use, facilitators may want to consider the topical focus for learning and numerous contextual variables, such as the number of teachers involved, the amount of time allocated for learning, and the availability of

TABLE 2.4 Sampling of Designs to Promote Staff Reflection
and Learning

Action research	"Action research is a form of disciplined inquiry that . . . can be as simple as raising a question about some educational practice and collecting information to answer the question, or can be as complicated as applying a *t*-Test to determine whether or not post-test results from an experimental group are statistically significant" (Glanz, 1999, p. 22).
Cadres	"Cadres are small groups that coalesce around specific issues, research options, and recommended course of action" (Rapaport, 1999, p. 24).
Cases	"Case-based professional development involves using carefully chosen, real-world examples of teaching to serve as springboards for discussion among small groups of teachers" (Barnett, 1999, p. 26).
Coaching	"Coaching provides a model of respectful collegial reflection about instructional decisions" (Harwell-McKee, 1999, p. 28).
Examining student work	Examining student work involves "structured conversations about the assignments teachers give to students, the standards students must achieve, and student work" (Mitchell, 1999, p. 32).
Journaling	"Journal writing . . . [is] a place for learners to record observations, toy with various perspectives, analyze their own practice, interpret their understanding of topics, keep records, make comments, or reconstruct experiences" (Killion, 1999, p. 36).
Mentoring	Mentoring "provides the newcomer with support, guidance, feedback, problem-solving guidance, and a network of colleagues who share resources, insights, practices, and materials" (Robbins, 1999, p. 40).
Portfolios	A portfolio is "a collection of items . . . gathered over time which forms the basis for discussion by colleagues or members of a group" (Dietz, 1999, p. 45).
Shadowing students	"Shadowing is the process of following a student and systematically recording that student's instructional experiences. The technique . . . provides a rich display of what happens in the classroom and provides a deeper understanding of the connection between pedagogy and student performance" (Wilson & Corbett, 1999, p. 47).

TABLE 2.4 Continued

Study groups	Study groups involve "a small number of individuals joining together to increase their capacities through new learning for the benefit of students" (Murphy & Lick, 1998, p. 4).
Tuning protocols	Tuning protocols involve "a group of colleagues coming together to examine each other's work, honor the good things found in that work, and fine tune it through a formal process of presentation and reflection" (Easton, 1999, p. 54).

SOURCE: All the excerpted definitions cited in Table 2.4 are from articles in the Summer 1999, *Journal of Staff Development* feature issue titled "Powerful Designs for Learning." Contact the National Staff Development Council for additional information (www.nsdc.org).

resource materials. Readers are encouraged to obtain the "Powerful Designs," Summer 1999 issue of the JSD as a resource when deciding on specific designs to promote reflection and learning.

Closing

The opportunities for educators to reflect on and learn from practice are limitless. Every experience presents an opportunity for growth, and even the most accomplished educators can improve their practices. With ongoing development of our personal capacities to create trusting relationships and to expand our thinking and inquiry, we can achieve high levels of competence and effectiveness as reflective educators. Ultimately, reflective practice becomes part of our core values and beliefs, which are central to any sustained development by individuals or organizations (Butler, 1996). We come to view ourselves as reflective educators. Being reflective becomes part of our identity. As long as we are reflecting, we are learning. As long as we are learning, we are growing. As long as we are growing, we are moving closer to our human potential for contributing to this world in our chosen role as educators. Despite the prevailing norms of isolation and the hectic pace of life in schools, we can feel optimistic about the potential of reflective practice to transform schools into communities in which educators and students embrace continuous learning and improvement.

You are invited to use the Chapter Reflection: Capturing Your Thoughts form on the next page (Figure 2.3) to make note of significant learning or insights sparked from reading Chapter 2. The next four chapters provide considerations for and specific examples of how reflective practices can be initiated at the individual (Chapter 3), partner (Chapter 4), small-group (Chapter 5), and schoolwide (Chapter 6) levels of the reflective practice spiral.

Figure 2.3. Chapter Reflection: Capturing Your Thoughts

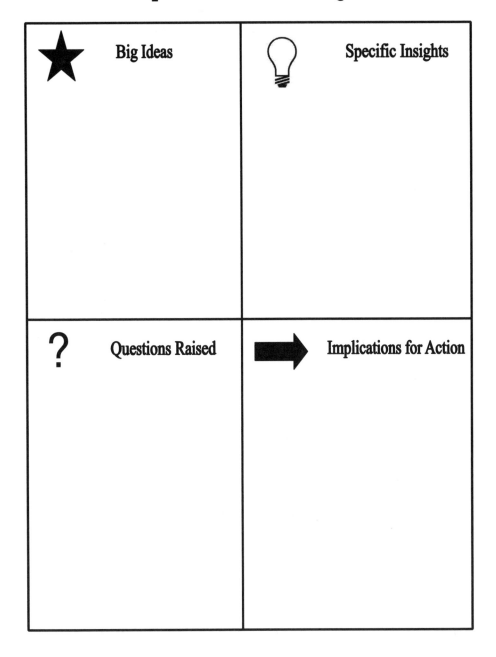

Individual Reflection

From the perspective of the individual teacher, it means that the
process of understanding and improving one's own teaching
must start from reflection on one's own experience.

—Kenneth M. Zeichner (1993, p. 8)
*Connecting Genuine Teacher Development
to the Struggle for Social Justice*

The place to begin with reflective practice is with yourself—the only part of the reflective practice spiral (Figure 3.1) over which you have control and for which you have total responsibility. Think about the life-saving advice offered to passengers before each flight on a commercial airline. You are instructed to put on your oxygen mask first so that you may better assist others. The greater your personal reflective capacities and practices, the greater your potential to influence colleagues in your school by participating—in partnership, small groups, and school-wide activity—as depicted in the reflective practice spiral. Others are drawn to and respect individuals who are thoughtful, who strive to continuously improve their practice, who are flexible in their approaches to teaching and learning, and who stay clearly focused on what matters most—students learning well. Self-development is the core of professional development or, "more profoundly, [it is the process of] personal being and becoming" (Butler, 1996, p. 265).

"Much of what happens in teaching is unknown to the teacher . . . and experience is insufficient as a basis for development" (Richards & Lockhart, 1994, pp. 3-4). To make the subtleties of our practice known and to develop new insights and understandings, we must choose a reflective stance about our practice. Becoming more reflective is the foundation for continuous development as an educator. Recall from Chapter 1 (see page 13) the positive gains that can be realized at the

Figure 3.1. The Reflective Practice Spiral With Individual Level of Reflection Highlighted

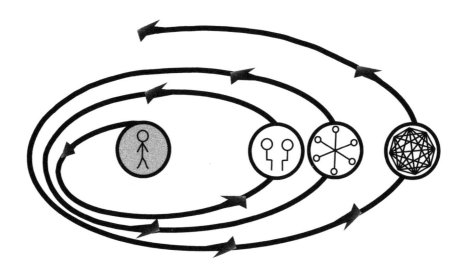

individual level in the reflective practice spiral. Reflection is guided by action, and action is guided by reflection.

This chapter and the following three chapters (Chapters 4 to 6) focus on the *how* of reflective practice and are organized in a parallel way. First, the level of reflective practice (i.e., individual, partners, small groups, entire school) is briefly reintroduced, referencing the initial introduction in Chapter 1. Next, considerations that are unique to the respective level of reflective practice are presented. These are followed by a description of examples from the world of practice and then a menu of additional ideas to consider for application. In reviewing the examples and ideas, you may recognize the potential for application at other levels in the reflective practice spiral. Each chapter closes with questions to assist you in getting started with reflective practice at that particular level. Many of the examples and ideas in Chapters 3 through 6 offer structures to promote reflective practice, but without understanding how to create reflective learning experiences within the structures, success is less likely. Changes in structure provide only the opportunity for meaningful changes in practice. Results depend on what happens within the structures. As you consider applications, we recommend reviewing Chapter 2 for more specific information about meaningful topics on which to reflect, values and principles of adult learning that should be honored, and individual capacities to be developed for reflection. This information provides the foundation for successful application of the examples and ideas presented in Chapters 3 through 6.

Special Considerations for Reflecting on Our Own

Perhaps the most important consideration for reflecting on your own is to recognize the difficulty of honoring your personal commitment to reflective practice. Our surrounding culture does little to support time-out for thinking and learning, particularly time alone. It can be viewed as unproductive and even selfish. Creating the space in which to think conflicts with the norms of doing. Given an unsupportive culture, it can be difficult to give yourself permission to reflect and learn. When you find yourself wavering, remember, "It is in the quiet and solitary times of reading and writing that the insights from life take on a more systematic form" (Webb, 1995, p. 76). To this we would add an emphasis on the thinking element of reading, writing, or whatever other mode of reflection works best for you.

You will find your own way of creating space for reflection. Some people mark time on their weekly calendars. Others build thinking space into daily routines—going for an early morning run, walking immediately after work, listening to audiotapes on a long commute, or journaling after the children are in bed. Beginning the day with a settled mind creates a state of presence and openness, which are requisites for reflection. Like exercise, we know reflective practice is good for us, but the commitment is difficult to sustain. This is one reason we have found that it is often easier to maintain a regular schedule of reflection when we are partnered with another person (see Chapter 4). It is sometimes easier to honor a commitment to other people than one made to ourselves.

Several considerations relate specifically to the process of developing reflective capacities within yourself. First, it is difficult to see circumstances in different ways. Our conclusions about past experiences inform our present thoughts and thereby limit, as much as inform, our perceptions. Our own view of the world is so much a part of who we are that it serves as a filter on our thinking. We must become aware of our biases and make a conscious effort to attempt seeing things from another perspective. We can ask ourselves

- What are some other ways of thinking about this?

- Has this always been the case, or have there been times when something different has happened? Why?

- What influences on thinking and behaving have I not considered?

- How do my beliefs guide me to think this way, and how might other beliefs alter my thinking?

- If I trusted people's intentions, would I interpret their responses differently?

- Are there other people who could help me see this differently?

- Why do I hold on so strongly to this one view?

Another challenge in learning to reflect on your own is finding your voice (Canning, 1991; Costa & Kallick, 2000b). We can fall into routine ways of doing things. We can also become accustomed to others telling us directly or implying indirectly what we should do. The busier we are, the more likely these things are to happen. Our hierarchical orientation in education supports expertness and can diminish recognizing and valuing our own wisdom. "Self-knowledge involves *what* and *how* you are thinking, even unconsciously. Many people are not used to engaging in the 'self-talk' that is necessary for hearing their inner voice" (Costa & Kallick, 2000b, p. 60).

Finally, like every other set of skills and dispositions, reflection capacities develop and become more integrated into how we think and who we are over time. Reflecting on your own is a good place to begin developing the individual capacities identified in Chapter 2: Be present, be open, listen without judgment and with empathy, seek understanding, assume mutuality in learning, honor the person, question, respond, and create dialogue. You can practice all of these capacities on your own, then carry them with you into learning conversations with others.

Reflecting on Our Own: Examples From Practice

In this section, we offer several frameworks (i.e., mental models) that have been used to prompt reflection at the individual level. They may be especially helpful in guiding early, intentional reflection experiences. Eventually, all of us develop our own way of prompting inquiry and reflection about our practice. The first two examples (A 4-Step Reflection Process and Letting Your Reflections Flow) were formatted on single pages and placed in faculty mailboxes in a school that was beginning a reflective practice initiative. These mailbox prompts, as they were called, served as gentle reminders to take a time-out for reflection and offered a structure for engaging in reflection.

A 4-Step Reflection Process

The 4-step reflection process outlined in Table 3.1 guides reflection-*on*-action and reflection-*for*-action, both focused around a specific event or circumstance. It brings the reflector through a sequenced process of thinking: description (what?), analysis and interpretation (why?), overall determination of meaning (so what?), and projections about future actions (now what?). This sequence of thinking is easily embedded into a personal reflection repertoire.

TABLE 3.1 A 4-Step Process for Guiding Reflection

Think about a significant event or interaction or lesson that occurred in your classroom or school—with students or adults—that you feel is worth further reflection. You might choose to examine a positive and encouraging experience, or you might choose a more unsettling and challenging experience.

Now consider the following series of questions to prompt your thinking about the experience. You may wish to write down your thoughts. You may even want to share your thoughts aloud with another person.

1. What happened? (Description)
   - What did I do? What did others (e.g., students, adults) do?
   - What was my affect at the time? What was their affect?
   - What was going on around us? Where were we? When during the day did it occur? Was there anything unusual happening?

2. Why? (Analysis, interpretation)
   - Why do I think things happened in this way?
   - How come I chose to act the way I did? What can I surmise about why the other person acted as she or he did? What was going on for each of us?
   - What was I thinking and feeling? Or was I thinking at the time? How might this have affected my choice of behavior?
   - How might the context have influenced the experience? Was there something about the activities? Something about the timing or location of events?
   - Are there other potential contributing factors? Something about what was said or done by others that triggered my response? Are there past experiences—mine or the school's—that may have contributed to the response?
   - What are my hunches about why things happened in the way they did?

3. So what? (Overall meaning and application)
   - Why did this seem like a significant event to reflect on?
   - What have I learned from this? How could I improve?
   - How might this change my future thinking, behaving, interactions?
   - What questions remain?

4. Now what? (Implications for action)
   - Are there other people I should actively include in reflecting on this event? If so, who and what would we interact about?
   - Next time a situation like this presents itself, what do I want to remember to think about? How do I want to behave?
   - How could I set up conditions to increase the likelihood of productive interactions and learning?

Letting Your Reflections Flow

David Bohm (1989) refers to dialogue as "a stream of meaning flowing among us and through us and between us" (p. 1). Although dialogue is often used to refer to interactions between people, it can also refer to a person's internal exploration of various viewpoints and assumptions—an inner dialogue. Most of us must learn how to dialogue with ourselves. It is not an intrinsic skill to any of us, although we each have the potential. Following are several different prompts for engaging in dialogue with yourself. Before you begin, you may wish to review the introductory description on dialogue located in Chapter 2 (pages 30-33). A recommended mode for dialogue with yourself is writing. However, be careful not to pressure yourself to write in technically correct ways. The purpose is expression of thought, not coherent and carefully sequenced articulation. The third prompt below poses an opportunity for freewriting, which is a way of brainstorming on paper. This form of writing is good practice for just letting thoughts flow onto paper. Select a prompt, and let the dialogue begin.

Have a written dialogue with yourself about what it means to be a teacher. When did you first think about being a teacher? What influenced your thinking in this way? Did particular teachers or other people influence your thoughts about becoming a teacher? How do you want to contribute to the lives of children? What are your hopes and visions? What do you want students to learn from you and with you? What do you need to continue learning from them? What are the underlying beliefs and values that guide your teaching? Where do you struggle with alignment between beliefs and values and actual behavior? Why? Explore potential reasons for this. How do you want to be as a teacher? What do you want to learn more about that will enhance your teaching? How can you remain true to these desires?

Identify a specific event or experience and write about it from as many perspectives as possible. What happened from my viewpoint? What happened from the viewpoint of others? How might someone in the balcony look down on and interpret the event? How can I make sense of what happened without turning the other person into the bad guy? Is there a way I can step into others' shoes? How can I view this as understandable difference instead of trying to identify winners and losers? Does there have to be a right way and wrong way?

Select any topic and do some freewriting. You may want to think metaphorically. Learning to reflect is like planting a seed, patiently watching it, and hoeing away the competing and unwanted weeds. For example, Bohm's depiction of dialogue as a stream of meaning could be envisioned as a river. Dialogue is like a river. Or teaching is like planting and tending a garden. Write down your thoughts, feelings, beliefs, and observations about the selected topic. Write about connections between your topic and other things. Do a quick spilling out of anything that

Figure 3.2. Reflection Directions

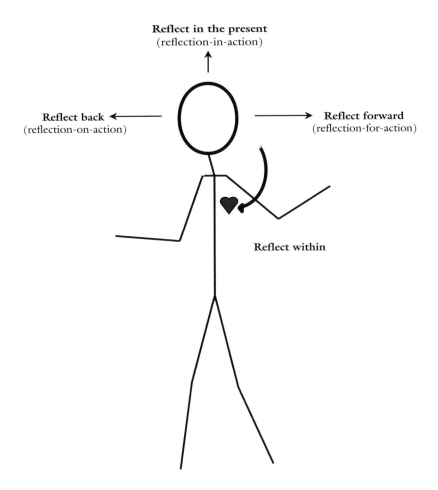

comes to your mind. Don't evaluate or judge thoughts as they pour out. Just let them flow! Later, look back at all your thoughts and connections. Ask yourself, "I wonder what this means? What are the connections between this and that? Are there new insights or perspectives I hadn't really thought about before? How did this experience of freeing up my mind expand my thinking? What additional questions are raised?"

Reflection Directions

Reflection has direction. Figure 3.2 depicts four different directions that guide reflection. As you begin or extend your process of individual reflection, practice these different ways of reflecting. You can reflect within to inquire about personal purpose and why you are the way you are. Why are you a teacher? How did you come to be here? What are your intentions? How do you stay centered? What nurtures your creativity and zest for teaching? How do you want to be with your students and colleagues?

You can reflect back on circumstances or events that have already occurred, referred to as reflection-on-action (Schon, 1983; Webb, 1995). This is one of the most frequently employed forms of reflection. It occurs after an event, when you are removed from it, and the doing is done (temporarily). The mind is then freed up to reflect on the *doing*.

> During [reflection-on-action], personal experiences are reflected on, a re-evaluation occurs. . . . During this activity, new data are linked to what is already known, relationships within the data are established, ideas and feelings are tested for their authenticity, and thus new personal practical knowledge and understanding are established. The outcome of this is the state for the design of future action; in other words, it is the input for reflection to action. (Butler, 1996, p. 274)

You can reflect in the present as events are occurring, referred to as reflection-in-action (Butler, 1996; Schon, 1983). This is one of the most difficult but potentially powerful forms of reflection. It is difficult because of the hot-action nature of teaching (see Eraut, 1985, quotation in Chapter 1). It is powerful because it is the means for making adjustments in the process of teaching, based on a keen awareness of what is going on in the present.

> Reflection-in-action . . . is possible if and only if there is mental processing capacity available to get outside the act of generation of the performance and to watch its effects and evaluate them. This means being able to accumulate and evaluate immediate feedback within the performance context . . . it allows modification of the performance plan to make it more efficacious. (Butler, 1996, p. 273)

The abilities to reflect in action and to make adjustments accordingly are readily apparent in master teachers. The mind of the master teacher is not totally consumed with delivering instruction and keeping students engaged. The mind of the master teacher is freed up to observe student responses, to notice subtle indicators of confusion, to identify unusual responses. Reflection-in-action requires a high level of consciousness. High-performing athletes also offer salient examples of reflection-in-action, making minor adjustments as they perform. Teachers consider, How are students responding? Who is not responding? When did student engagement trail off? Why?

You can reflect forward, referred to as reflection-*for*-action or reflection-*to*-action (Butler, 1996). In this type of reflection, you envision the effect of specific actions or interventions on a group of students, the classroom as a whole, a group of colleagues, the learning environment, and the school as a community. Reflection-for-action has the potential to identify future ways of thinking or behaving that are likely to produce desirable results. As mentioned above, reflection-on-action is the major input source for considering reflection-for-action.

Five States of Mind

The five states of mind described by Costa and Garmston (1994) offer another framework or mental model for guiding reflection on your own. Briefly described below are each of the five states of mind, with related questions that prompt reflection:

- *Efficacy* involves having an internal locus of control and knowing that you can make a difference. "Am I thinking efficaciously in this situation? How am I assuming responsibility for my role in this situation?"

- *Flexibility* involves thinking outside the box, choosing to look at things from a different perspective. "Am I thinking flexibly, or am I limited to only one way of thinking?"

- *Craftsmanship* is a focus on continuous improvement, a desire to always get better at what you do. "Is this better than what we or I used to do? How can it be improved?"

- *Consciousness* is being aware of your own process of thinking; the contexts or environments around you; and the relationships among various thoughts, actions, and circumstances. "What am I aware of? What is not here that needs to be? What don't I know?"

- *Interdependence* recognizes that you are never working alone, because you are always involved in an interdependent relationship whether you want to be or not. "Who else might help? Who else is or might be involved? What would my friend Diane do?"

Thinking through this framework prompts internal reflection that can assist getting unstuck when what we are doing isn't working. Thinking through the situation and considering each of the states of mind usually results in a pathway opening up. One of the authors of this book has the five states of mind posted on the wall in his office. When stuck, he looks at the posted states of mind and goes down the list, one by one, thinking about the problem, his actions so far, and what he may have forgotten to try. Sometimes, it is important to look for what is not there as much as what is there. Thinking about the questions posed above prompt reflection-on-action and reflection-for-action.

Reflecting on Our Own: More Ideas to Consider

There are many creative ways to reflect that people have discovered for themselves. Not everyone benefits from prompts or prescribed processes, such as those described above. Some find that meditation and prayer open their minds and hearts to different ways of thinking. For others, exercise or music has the effect of creating space for new thoughts and insights to emerge. Still others listen to audiotaped books as a way to both ground and expand thinking about practice. We even know of individuals who simply go to sleep and let their unconscious minds take over the processing of problems or complexities of practice, later resulting in more conscious insights or understandings. Oftentimes, they wake up in the middle of the night with clear minds and new ideas. Undoubtedly, we are on the front end of discovering myriad ways to enrich and expand our thinking capacities, which will unleash exponentially our ways of doing. Below is a menu of ideas for reflecting on your own that may spark an interest for you.

Journaling

Journaling makes the invisible thoughts visible. It provides a means of describing practice as well as identifying and clarifying beliefs, perspectives, challenges, and hopes for practice. It is a way to put your thoughts down on paper. It offers a private place for honest accounting and review. You can go back and read entries many times. It sometimes helps to recall thoughts and different times in your life. If you have journaled about past problems, when you face another, you may be able to find references, analogies, and solving strategies that have worked previously. Journaling is quiet, reflective time alone. A middle school principal once explained that journaling was a way to dump thoughts and feelings, which helped him get rid of old problems. He was able to write about an issue, to think about it, and then to let it go. He also used his journal as a way to document events.

Some people use a carefully chosen, beautiful journal. Some use Post-it notes. Others use whatever loose sheets of paper might be available, then deposit the written-on papers in a place in which the writing can be reviewed at a later time. "[M]aking entries in confidential journals can help us as teachers see where we divert from our lesson plans, what procedures seem to work well for students, which activities are less successful, and so on" (Bailey, Curtis, & Nunan, 1998, p. 549). Entries in journals can include various items, such as date and time, a short description of what happened (with greater detail given about important aspects of an event), and an analysis (Posner, 1996). The significance and implications may be included as well. Benefits of journaling have been identified as expanding awareness, understanding, and insights about teaching practice; making connections between theory and practice; and generating new hypotheses for action (Taggart & Wilson, 1998). Journaling helps to clarify your thinking. It can also be done using an interactive format with partners (see Chapter 4).

Mapping

Mapping could be considered a form of journaling. Journaling is a linear or sequential presentation of written information—one sentence or thought after another. Mapping is a more fluid presentation, showing connections and relationships between ideas and information. Similar to graphic organizing, mapping is a way to visually represent an event, meeting, lesson, curricular unit, reading, or presentation. A map can clearly communicate the big ideas at a glance. For example, a presenter may have shared and expanded on three main ideas about classroom management: relationships, classroom expectations, and communication structures. Figure 3.3 illustrates how a map of that presentation may have looked. Mapping allows different emphases on information by altering the sizes, boldness, accents, and locations of words and pictures. It also easily depicts relationships among the main ideas as well as between each main idea and its respective subpoints. The process of constructing maps requires higher-order thinking about the content and creates a framework onto which future information can be added.

Teacher Narratives

Teacher narratives are "stories written by and about teachers that form the basis of narrative inquiry" (Sparks-Langer & Colton, 1991, p. 42). They are a somewhat more-disciplined form of writing than journaling. Journaling is more free flowing. Teacher narratives usually have more structure and focus, because their intent is to communicate a story. Either keen observers or teachers themselves write real stories about teaching. The stories illuminate the realities, dilemmas, joys, and rewards of teaching. Reflecting on teacher narratives yields several benefits: insights about motivations for teacher actions, about the details and complexities of teaching, and about teachers themselves (Sparks-Langer & Colton, 1991).

Teacher narratives can be specifically designed for use as case studies, in which specific problems of practice that require reflection for analysis and solution finding would be accentuated. Case studies have the advantage of portraying realities of practice without requiring in vivo observations, which are time-consuming (Taggart & Wilson, 1998). Autobiographical sketches, also called personal histories (Sparks-Langer & Colton, 1994), are a specialized form of teacher narratives (Taggart & Wilson, 1998). The stories are of a more personal and in-depth nature, offering insight "into the past to uncover preconceived theories about teaching and learning" (Taggart & Wilson, 1998, p. 164).

Figure 3.3. Sample Reflection Map on a Presentation About Classroom Management

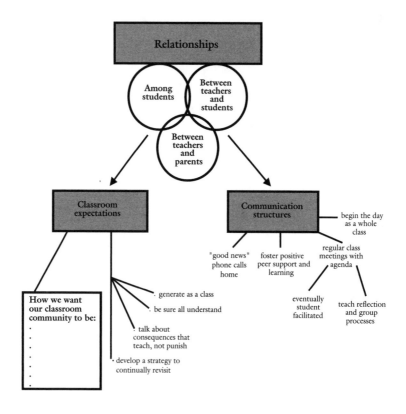

Teaching Portfolios

Teaching portfolios have been described as "a purposeful collection of any aspect of a teacher's work that tells the story of a teacher's efforts, skills, abilities, achievements, contributions to students, colleagues, institution, academic discipline or community" (Brown & Wolfe-Quintero, 1997, p. 28). Items that might be included in a teaching portfolio (Bailey, Curtis, & Nunan, 1998) are (a) a personal statement of teaching philosophy, strengths, interests, challenges; (b) a description of teaching goals and responsibilities (e.g., courses, specific assignments); (c) any materials developed by the teacher (e.g., lesson plans, syllabi, assignments, audiovisuals, tests); and (d) evidence about teaching performance and effectiveness (e.g., student feedback, student-performance data, colleague and peer perspectives, supervisor feedback) and the teacher's interpretation or analysis of the evidence.

Teaching portfolios offer numerous assets for the process of reflection (Bailey et al., 1998; Brown & Wolfe-Quintero, 1997). First, the process of reviewing and selecting items for the portfolio is itself a reflective process. "The very process of developing a portfolio can help [teachers] gather together their thoughts about their professional strengths and synthesize them into a cogent collage" (Brown & Wolfe-Quintero, 1997, p. 29). Second, teaching portfolios contain multiple and varied data about teaching and its effects. They provide multiple perspectives that add breadth and depth to the analysis process. Third, the time spent reflecting on the teaching portfolio as a whole "inevitably enlarges a teacher's view of what teaching is" (Brown & Wolfe-Quintero, 1997, p. 29). Finally, teaching portfolios provide one way of documenting the nature of one's teaching at one point in time. In reviewing portfolios over the years, one realizes one's growth. Use of teaching portfolios not only serves to document growth but also contributes to it.

Instead of creating a comprehensive portfolio that addresses an entire scope of teaching, smaller portfolios that focus on one specific area of teaching (e.g., one course or curricular area) could be developed. This allows a focused review of specific areas and facilitates an easier revision process, because the materials for each area are gathered together. Another idea is to include a partner in the portfolio's design and review process, in the same way that a teacher assists a student in portfolio design, selection, and review. Another person adds the invaluable dimension of an outside perspective and offers a coach to support the reflection and inquiry process.

Metaphors

Metaphorical thinking is a way of illuminating features through comparison. It has been described as

> Attending to likenesses, to relationships, and to structural features . . . identifying conceptual categories that may not be obvious or previously acknowledged . . . making knowledge in one domain a guide for comprehending knowledge in another, with some transfer or meaning taking place in both directions. . . . To be a metaphorical thinker is to be a constructive learner, one who actively builds bridges from the known to the new. (Pugh, Hicks, Davis, & Venstra, 1992, pp. 4-5)

Metaphors can be used to simplify and clarify problems, summarize thoughts, develop alternative ways of thinking about a topic or event, and communicate abstract ideas (Taggart & Wilson, 1998). "A metaphor holds the most meaning in the smallest space" (source unknown).

Johnston (1994) described one example of the use of metaphor to promote reflection. She requested that each of three students completing a masters program "write a metaphor that described her experience in the program, paying particular attention to capturing ways in which she had changed or not changed during the two years" (p. 15). One student wrote about being a contractor, explaining that initially she followed predesigned plans but that over time, she and the future home owners worked together to create customized plans. Another student wrote about being a tree in a drought, whose roots system had to seek out new sources of nutrients. The third student captured her experience as an artichoke with each petal being an element of practice that can be understood only when peeled away and examined. (Use of metaphors to promote reflection in the context of groups and teams is presented in Chapter 5.)

Reading With Reflection

Ideas for individual reflection would be incomplete without emphasizing the value of reading and reflecting on the information. Although one emphasis of reflective practice is frequently on generating internal knowledge and making sense of one's teaching practice, much can be learned from outside sources of knowledge. Given the isolating tendencies in the teaching profession, such as teaching in the same school or district for one's entire career, educators particularly must make concerted efforts to stay informed about findings from research and about practices occurring elsewhere in education. There are many ways to teach and learn. The greater one's repertoire, the greater the likelihood for success with all students.

The amount of professional literature is overwhelming. Fortunately, much of it is now readily accessed electronically. Subscriptions to leading professional journals result in current literature conveniently delivered to your doorstep. Although there may be little time to read volumes of information, scanning for particularly relevant articles and using a highlighter or making notes in the margins can accentuate significant learning. Keeping Post-it notes close by facilitates jotting down key ideas and transferring them to a calendar or plan book for application or follow-up. Also, listening to professional publications and presentations on audiotape in the car is convenient.

Reading professional literature is one important source for new information, ideas, and insights. It is an important source of continuous professional learning and helps to renew teachers and keep their teaching fresh.

Getting Started With Reflection on Your Own

The decision to be a reflective educator is a commitment to your own growth and demonstrates a high level of personal responsibility and leadership for continuous improvement in educational practice. It is how you develop the expertise and insights that accumulate in wisdom. It is a commitment made in a life context that reluctantly yields space for thinking and creating. We are confident that it is a decision you will not regret. In fact, we believe that becoming more reflective is likely to heighten your awareness of the deep-seated yearning to make sense of your world and become the best you can be. Webb (1995) describes the paradox of subtle urgency for reflection in our life of practice:

> Reflection-on-action remains the endangered species of reflective practice. It is the most easily lost due to pressure of work and its loss has no immediate, transparent effect. My experience continues to tell me, however, that the quiet times of reflection-on-action are critical for the survival of my own reflective practice . . . this puts the onus on one's self to make the time and organize one's life in such a way that reflection-on-action can continue to have an impact on professional practice. (p. 77)

The longest relationship that you have is with yourself. Why not make the best of it! Becoming more reflective is a way to learn more about who you are, what is important to you, how you think, what you say and do, and how you are as an educator. Choosing reflection supports your desire for high-quality performance.

To further guide your thinking about developing your own style of reflection, we invite you to contemplate the following questions:

- Thinking about your own development as an educator, what are you most interested in learning more about? Why does this seem important to you?

- As you reflect on your daily practice, what are your biggest questions? In what aspects of the curriculum are students not quite getting it? How could you maximize the learning strengths of all your students?

- What would be the best way to go about addressing these interests and questions? What means of reflection are best aligned with your learning styles (e.g., journaling, exercising, reading, mapping)?

- How might you create space in your life to reflect and learn on a regular basis?

- Are there additional people you want to include in your process of reflection?

The Chapter Reflection: Capturing Your Thoughts form (Figure 3.4) on the next page can be used to jot down your thoughts in response to these questions.

You can genuinely teach only who you are (Palmer, 1998). In these demanding times, it is easy to slide to a place of feeling as if you are never enough. But who you are everyday, how you create meaningful learning experiences for students, the positive energy you choose to bring to your work is enough. It is more than enough: It is an enormous gift to the world around you. By maintaining a focus on reflective capacities that expand and improve your personal practices, your influence on others expands as well. Just remember to place your own oxygen mask securely in place before assisting others.

Figure 3.4. Chapter Reflection: Capturing Your Thoughts

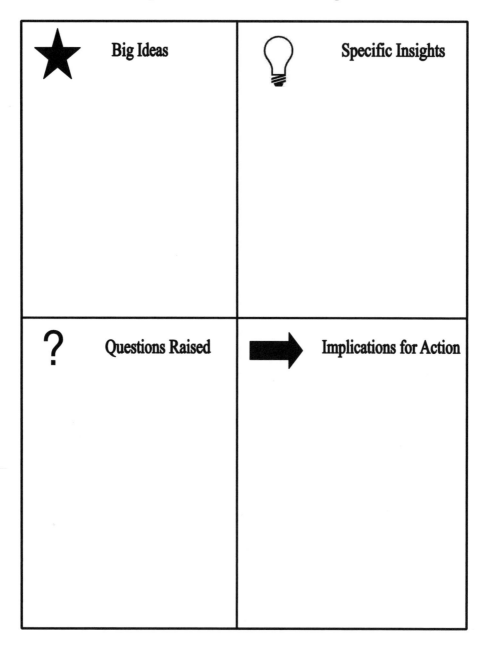

$$4$$

Reflection With Partners

Awareness of one's own intuitive thinking usually
grows out of practice in articulating it to others.

—Donald Schon (1983, p. 243)
*The Reflective Practitioner: How
Professionals Think in Action*

A s human beings, we are drawn to interactions with others. These interactions provide a means of understanding who we are in our world around us—our professional and personal lives. Reflecting on educational practice with another person has the potential to greatly enrich our understanding and to support improvements in our practice (Costa & Kallick, 2000b). Because we filter our experiences through our own views of the world, reflecting alone can result in self-validation and justification (Bright, 1996; Butler, 1996; Levin, 1995; Zeichner, 1993). Reflection with another offers a safeguard against perpetuating only our own thoughts. Bright (1996) explains,

> Because it is the practitioner's understanding which is the window through which a situation is understood and interpreted, an essential feature of 'reflective practice' is the need for the practitioner to be aware of her own processes in the development and construction of this interpretation . . . to understand how she understands a situation. . . . As intimated earlier, 'reflective practice' is not easy, and the 'self-reflexive' element of it makes it even more difficult. Paradoxically, this suggests the role of others in this self-reflective process because colleagues and clients may be very perceptive in detecting assumptions and bias present within a practitioner's practice. (pp. 177-178)

Figure 4.1. The Reflective Practice Spiral With Partner Level of Reflection Highlighted

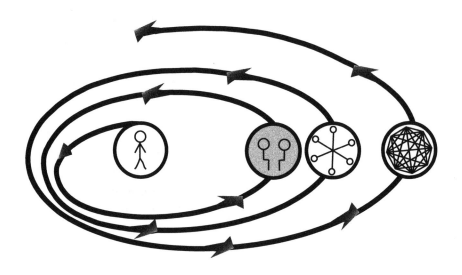

During reflection, a partner assists us in gaining awareness of fixed assumptions and viewing events from a second perspective (Bright, 1996; Butler, 1996). Reflecting with a partner addresses the major concern about reflecting solely with ourselves, which is solely reinforcing our own views and perceptions. Compared with reflection in groups, partner reflection offers the advantage of more privacy. Trust, therefore, is more readily fostered. Trust and safety are always issues when interacting with others. The fewer the people, the more easily trust is established.

Recall from Chapter 1 (see page 14) the potential gains that can be realized at the partner level in the reflective practice spiral (Figure 4.1). In addition to offering new insights, reflecting with a partner has the potential to strengthen collegial relationships, decrease feelings of isolation, and increase a sense of connection to one's place of work. Reflection with partners can increase skills and confidence in the reflective practice process, thereby bolstering courage and commitment to expand reflection to the arena of small groups (Chapter 5) or even schoolwide (Chapter 6)—the outer levels of the reflective practice spiral.

In this chapter, we focus on how to engage in reflective practices with partners. We use the term *reflection partners* to refer to two or three individuals (dyads or triads) who make a commitment to engage in a reflective learning process that is focused on improving educational practice and, therefore, student learning. We distinguish between reflection as partners and reflection in groups or teams (the next chapter) in the following ways. Partner groups are smaller and participation is almost always voluntary, which means that the individuals involved usually are self-directed and motivated to reflect together. They have connections through shared interests, areas of practice, or individual characteristics. In this chapter, we expand the how-to information shared in Chapter 4 (individual reflection) to include partners. Again, we offer considerations, examples, ideas, and suggestions for getting started with reflective practice at the partner level.

Special Considerations for Reflection Partners

Engaging in a reflective process with another person requires consideration of numerous factors. It is not safe to assume that adults who learn well by themselves will learn well with others. Think about the kind of specific support teachers provide to students when students are expected to work together compared with when they work on their own. So, too, adults must consider carefully how to construct successful, partnered learning experiences. Here we offer considerations related to the purpose of reflection, with whom to reflect, and ways to reflect together. All these considerations interact with one another. The desired focus of reflection influences who is selected as a reflection partner. Conversely, the choice of a reflection partner influences what to reflect on. The topical emphases for reflection are infinite; the reflection-partner options may not be as plentiful. For some people, the choice of a partner precedes identification of a specific reflection focus.

What Is the Purpose of Your Partner Reflection?

As with any type of reflection, the overarching purpose of the precious time spent with a partner is to expand your understanding about practice and your repertoire of effective interventions. Partner reflection may focus on a specific area of your teaching, a shared teaching situation (e.g., coteaching), or a specific aspect of your partner's teaching. You could also choose to reflect together on external information or circumstances (e.g., professional literature, a new curriculum, observations at another school).

Dyads and triads offer an excellent opportunity to inquire about the process of learning through reflection. How does the reflection process influence my thinking? What conditions are conducive to my reflection? What conditions inhibit my reflection? Why am I drawn to reflect on specific aspects of my teaching practice? How do I increase my reflection as I am teaching (reflection-in-action), instead of primarily afterward (reflection-on-action)? How are my personal reflection capacities (being present, being open, listening) developing? These questions are fundamental for continuous improvement of practice and are well suited for reflection with partners.

It is probably stating the obvious to emphasize that the topical focus of reflection should be something that is very important to you (see pages 33-37 in Chapter 2 for specific ideas). Otherwise, you are not likely to continue carving out time for partner reflection. If you are not learning or you are not learning about something that interests you, the time allocated for reflection will soon become filled with other activities. Time together learning is too valuable to be spent on issues of lesser importance or, worse, issues that detract from your growth (e.g., gossip, focusing on circumstances beyond your control).

The amount and type of teaching experience can also influence the focus of reflection (see pages 35-36 in Chapter 2). Early in one's career, the learning and improvement process usually concentrates on classroom management, working one's way through the curriculum, and delivery of instruction. Later on, the learning and improvement process expands to include more complex instructional issues (e.g., differentiating instruction to meet a wider range of abilities and interests), productive collaboration with colleagues, and efforts to initiate or continue schoolwide improvement efforts.

With Whom Might You Reflect?

It cannot be emphasized enough that for reflection to promote learning, you must be in a trusting relationship. Recall from Chapter 2 that trust provides the foundation for inquiry. To be in a trusting relationship, one has to be trustworthy. One indicator of trustworthiness is congruency between actions and words. Is there alignment between what one says and what one does? Ideal reflection partners are people who demonstrate such integrity, who are student centered, and who stay focused on their purpose as educators.

Most often, initial reflection partners are self-selected because the desire to reflect in dyads or triads is usually inside-out (self-initiated). Sometimes, partners are mandated (e.g., mentoring). An initial partner usually shares an interest in some aspects of practice as well as similar experiences and viewpoints. Over time, there may be a desire to learn with and from someone who has different experiences and views. In a trusting relationship with mutual respect, differences are honored, appreciated, and spark great growth potential. Choose to be with people who produce energy rather than drain it. Negativity and cynicism are not only unproductive, they diminish your spirit. You are not as alive as you could be. Seek people who are open to growth—yours and theirs. Be wary of people who have expert tendencies. No one knows it all. Everyone can improve.

Another consideration for the selection of reflection partners is very practical: access. How proximal is your potential partner? Long or stressful drives, for example, inhibit access. Are there common meeting times during the day or week that work well? How frequently do you and your partner want to meet? A checklist of considerations for partner selection is offered in Table 4.1. Of course, this list includes characteristics to continuously develop within oneself.

TABLE 4.1 Characteristics to Consider When Selecting a Reflective
Practice Partner

Essential characteristics: Those characteristics that I would choose to be present
in any reflective practice partner.

Someone who
___ stays focused on student learning.
___ is committed to continuous improvement.
___ is trustworthy.
___ contributes positively to the overall climate.
___ is a good listener.
___ is open to examining practice—hers and mine.
___ will inquire about and help expand my thinking.
___ will encourage and support changes in practice.
___ aligns actions and words.
___ is accessible enough to promote regular opportunities to reflect together.

Variable characteristics: Those characteristics that I may intentionally choose as
similar to or different from mine, depending on my learning needs and desires.

___ years of teaching experience
___ type of teaching experience (e.g., level, content area, school
    demographics)
___ teaching style and philosophy
___ life experience
___ age
___ gender
___ ethnicity, culture
___ personality
___ learning style

How Do You Reflect Together?

Early in the process of reflecting together, partners should articulate their
learning desires and needs. One way to do this is to take a few minutes individually
and then share responses to the following prompts: (a) "Something I would like to
learn more about is . . . because . . ."; (b) "Things that help me to be reflective are
. . . ." The first prompt identifies potential content emphases for reflection. It may
also result in targeting personal reflection capacities for improvement (described in
Chapter 2): for example, "I would like to get better at listening without feeling the
need to respond." The second prompt gets at conditions that promote reflection,
ranging from the surrounding environment (e.g., noise level, light, temperature,

seating arrangements) to ways of interacting (e.g., needing time to process before responding).

At the beginning of reflective interactions, partners might clarify what they think they want from the interaction. For example, is the purpose to obtain insight, to identify a range of options, to make a decision, or to just get things out and clarify issues? At the end of each interaction, it can be helpful to recap the ground traveled and to articulate areas of greatest significance. Sample formats for closing reflections are offered in Figure 5.6 on page 98 in Chapter 5.

Between the start and end of a session, the focus of reflection is inquiry. One strategy that has proven successful for promoting inquiry is coaching (Costa & Garmston, 1994).

> The student cannot be taught what he needs to know, but he can be coached; he has to see on his own behalf and in his own way the relations between means and methods employed and results achieved. Nobody else can see for him, and he can't see just by being "told," although the right kind of telling may guide his seeing and thus help him see what he needs to see. (Schon, 1987, p. 14)

You may wish to refer to the questioning, responding, and dialogue sections in Chapter 2 (pages 26-33) for specific strategies that promote inquiry and thinking. The reflection frameworks that were offered in Chapter 3 (pages 46-51) might also be useful.

Consistently referred to in the literature on reflective practice is the need for frame breaking, which is the process of coming to view things in another way, from a different viewpoint, or within a new framework. This is not easy, in part because it can be uncomfortable. Butler (1996) explains, "To dislodge personal theories, to break the framework for understandings that govern personal and professional performance and to create newer versions involves, necessarily, a period of discomfort" (p. 276). Here are two recent examples that illustrate both the difficulty of and the need for frame breaking. The first example involved a small group of teachers who visited another school to observe a more integrated and collaborative approach for teaching special education students and second-language learners. Several returned from the visit feeling frustrated. They indicated that they did not learn anything that could be applied to their specific circumstances. They quickly identified differences between their school and the school they visited in terms of school size, student population, and staff complement. These differences blocked their ability to see the classroom level practices of differentiated instruction and coteaching. The second example involved a group of paraprofessionals who were being taught how to support students with disabilities to do more for themselves. For example, instead of the paraprofessionals gathering and preparing all the materials for an instructional activity, they were instructed on how to prompt students to prepare for the activities without adult assistance. One paraprofessional responded, "We don't have to learn how to do this because we already do those things for the students." In other words, because the paraprofessionals did not view the students as capable of independence, they saw no need to teach the students to participate in activity preparation.

Different experiences and tightly held views block individuals from learning new ways of thinking and practice. Frequently, another person is needed to coach different ways of thinking about specific situations (examples follow in the next section). For learning to take place, ultimately, firmly entrenched viewpoints must be let go. "Learning is and should be, on some occasions, a disturbing and unsettling process . . . deep learning involves frame breaking and discomfort" (Butler, 1996, pp. 275-276).

To assist in the process of frame breaking, Ross (1990) offers five elements of a reflective process that can structure a learning interaction between reflection partners:

- Recognizing educational dilemmas

- Responding to a dilemma by recognizing both the similarities to other situations and the unique qualities of the particular situation

- Framing and reframing the dilemma

- Experimenting with the dilemma to discover the implications of various solutions

- Examining the intended and unintended consequences of an implemented solution and evaluating whether the consequences are desirable

Some of the examples below illustrate this type of frame-breaking process. Also offered are additional frameworks or processes to structure reflection with partners.

Reflection Partners: Examples From Practice

In educational practice, partner reflection may be one of the most commonly used supports for continuous learning and improvement. Reflection as partners has the benefit of diversity in thought in relatively safe circumstances, because only a few individuals are involved. Described here are both formal and informal ways of reflecting with partners.

Reflective Voice Mail Bridges the Time Crunch

Voice mail was probably not envisioned as a mechanism for reflective practice, but for two authors of this book, it has unintentionally become a critical channel for ongoing partner reflection. On campus and in the public schools, the two of us are joined in a variety of interrelated activities and projects. We work both inde-pendently and interdependently on these shared endeavors. Sometimes, we need to communicate daily. As is common with many educators, we find it exceedingly difficult to find time to meet regularly. In the past couple of years, voice mail emerged as a productive and convenient communication and reflection link. We can access the voice-mail system at any time to record or review messages. We ini-tially used it only to leave updates and check-ins. Over time, we began using the voice-mail system to also share our perceptions, insights, and questions about events and what they meant for our project work. It became increasingly common for one of us to connect to the voice-mail system and have four new messages from the other. The reply feature of voice mail allows an immediate and easy way to respond. The save feature allows messages to be listened to again at a later time. The ability to have control over the wait time in between our messages allows us to think in a deeper, more integrated, and more creative manner about our shared work. Mes-sages are traded 24 hours a day. The instant that either of us has a thought or per-spective to share is the right time to leave a message.

Another noted benefit of voice mail is its singular sensory input. Because the voice-mail modality offers only auditory input, we are keenly aware of the intona-tion, affect, and emotional overtones. Because we do not feel the need to respond immediately, and we are not just waiting for a pause in which to add our perspec-tive, we listen more fully and with the intent of understanding.

Reflective Practice
in Paraprofessional Training and Teaming

An increasing number of paraprofessionals provide direct instruction to special education students. Most have received little or no training to do so. As a result, the training and supervision of paraprofessionals has become a common responsi-bility for many special educators (and other licensed teaching personnel). The fol-lowing example describes how and why one special educator focused on teaching paraprofessionals to be reflective in their work with students.

Evergreen High School is an urban high school with about 1,850 students, 30 of whom have physical disabilities and are supported by 3 special educators and 11 paraprofessionals. The students' programs are individualized because of their com-plex needs and multiple services. They attend general-education classes and a spe-cial education support class. Some are also involved in community-based instruc-tion. Shannon, one of the special educators, assumed primary responsibility for the paraprofessionals and decided to embed reflection in their ongoing work with stu-dents. Specifically, she felt that reflection was a way to (a) enhance the knowledge and skills of paraprofessionals to effectively support students with disabilities through-out the whole school day, and (b) create a culture within the special education team and supports questioning and reflecting on the best ways to support students with disabilities as the norm, not the exception, for all staff members.

Shannon developed and implemented a plan for supporting the development of paraprofessionals. She met with them individually, in small groups and as a whole group. The focus of individual meetings was on interacting about individual students, sharing specific information about how to teach a student, and reflecting on what was working well in specific classes, what wasn't, and why. If a specific need for training was identified, Shannon arranged for the paraprofessional to meet with the appropriate staff member to have this information taught or reviewed. Acknowledgment of the paraprofessionals' needs along with a show of respect for their input were significant influences on the development of a new culture that promoted reflection, sharing, and learning together. Also evident was a willingness to confront difficult issues. Greater trust and openness had emerged in the teacher-paraprofessional relationships.

Small-group meetings were held to discuss general instructional and support issues as well as specific student issues, as appropriate, among several paraprofessionals. One of the small-group meeting structures was referred to as Kid of the Day. Any teacher or paraprofessional could initiate a Kid of the Day meeting if there was an issue or concern about a student that needed to be discussed by the team. Staff members who worked with that student would get together to talk, share, reflect, and problem solve. In order to create time for Kid of the Day meetings, everyone (teachers and paraprofessionals) had to help cover other staff members' assignments for short periods.

Shannon scheduled meetings with the whole group of paraprofessionals every 2 to 3 weeks. She always had an agenda for the meeting, which the paraprofessionals helped to shape. At the beginning of the year, Shannon facilitated conversations to uncover assumptions held about students and about the responsibilities of paraprofessionals in supporting the students. Conversations covered showing respect for students and staff, including what respect looks like. At the trimester switch, concerns raised by the paraprofessionals dominated the agenda. For example, for paraprofessionals who worked with the same students, sharing student-specific information (e.g., individualized learning-support strategies, advocacy, communication styles and skills) became important.

All the meetings had three purposes. First, the paraprofessionals needed to learn specific strategies for supporting individual students in their respective classroom contexts. Second, they needed to develop a sense of being a team member who shares responsibility for overall program effectiveness. Third, they needed to develop clarity about the vision and philosophy of the program. Key questions were continually woven into conversations between Shannon and the paraprofessionals. What is the philosophy of the program? What do we want to see students doing and learning in their classes? How do we envision the students performing in the future? What are the expectations for the students? How does each of us contribute to a positive future for each student? How are students respectfully supported in their learning process? When do students need coaching, and when do they need direct instruction? Interacting around these types of reflective questions, participants developed a set of shared values and goals that served as a foundation for making decisions about practice.

Over the course of the first year, Shannon noticed that the paraprofessionals no longer just asked her questions about specific students and their programs; they also provided feedback and shared ideas with one another on how to work with a student. Both Shannon and the paraprofessionals have similar and clearer operating assumptions about the program and the individual students. Shannon now observes the paraprofessionals facilitating student responsibility and self-advocacy instead of doing too much for the students. She sees paraprofessionals as more thoughtful and reflective in their dealings with students. This provides a significant model for general-education teachers about how to work effectively with individual students. Shannon has also seen some of the paraprofessionals become more involved in other building-wide initiatives. Raising questions and learning together is becoming the norm rather than the exception.

Coaching: Three Examples

Cognitive coaching is a way to expand the thinking capacity of individuals so they create their own best ways to address issues. When someone chooses to be coached, the coach poses thoughtfully constructed questions to elicit that person's thinking. The five states of mind (see Costa & Garmston, 1994, Chapter 3, page 51) provide a framework for asking questions and offering responses. Following are three examples of coaching (which involved one of the authors of this book).

Coaching for Interdisciplinary Instruction

One summer day, two excellent high school teachers came into the scheduling office to talk to the assistant principal. They said they wanted to team teach. One taught biology and the other English. They wanted the same students during first and second hour so they could do some 2-hour instructional blocks. This was a very traditional school, organized around a traditional six-period day. Because the administrator had coached both of the teachers individually, he knew they were very effective teachers and great with students. Both were also very global thinkers.

After the teachers talked about their plan, the principal assumed a coaching role and inquired about specific aspects of implementation, that is, he asked them to reflect forward on their anticipated work together. He asked questions such as, "What are you going to do the first week of class?" "What are some of the common themes across your disciplines? For example, how is conflict evident in living systems and evident in written words?" The teachers had a great idea, and they knew the results they wanted for students, but they had not yet figured out how to get started. Attending to details was not a strength for either teacher. Throughout the summer, the principal and teachers met every couple of weeks for a brief coaching session. The teachers created a more specific instructional plan, and classes were scheduled back-to-back so the students would be together for two periods.

The principal and teachers met four times during the first trimester. Questions raised to promote thinking during the coaching sessions included, "How are you integrating the two content areas? How are you teaming together? What roles do each of you assume? How do you know you are making a difference for the kids? In what ways do you see the students making connections between biology and English? How are your relationships with your other colleagues?"

At the end of the first trimester, the principal asked them about the outcomes of their interdisciplinary venture. The English teacher said he was now teaching composition using the scientific method, and the biology teacher said he was now teaching science using journaling. Sometimes magic happens when you are able to facilitate putting people together, and you let learning happen.

Coaching to Reflect Back, Then Forward

One day, a foreign language teacher walked into the principal's office and asked for an hour of his time. She said, "You always give me great ideas." He was surprised, especially because he speaks only English. He was trying to remember any idea he suggested and said, "What idea have I given you?" After about a 30-second pause, she said, "Well, all I know is that I come out of our conversations with more ideas." The principal relaxed now, knowing that all he had to do was ask questions, not give ideas. He did not have the answers; she did. Coaching supports the seekers to come up with their own best ways.

The principal inquired about the year that had just finished. How did the results compare with what the teacher thought would happen? What influenced those results? What might make sense to start working on for the next year? These types of questions provided an opportunity for the teacher to reflect backward, inward, and forward. It is important to emphasize again that because the principal didn't speak a foreign language or teach it, the teacher was doing most of the thinking. The principal facilitated the reflection process by asking questions to help the teacher clarify her own thinking. In this situation, the coach's role was to ask questions that supported the teacher taking risks, generating new ideas, and reflecting on her practice.

Coaching to Promote Problem Solving

In a junior high school, a course in coaching for reflective thought was being offered to the staff. The principal, who was the instructor for the course, held an informational meeting before school started. The head custodian asked if he could attend. The principal was enthusiastic about the custodian participating. They knew each other from another building so trust was already established. The principal asked the custodian why he chose to sign up for coaching. The custodian said he had a lot of trouble controlling his temper, which the principal also had noted, although he valued him as a good custodian. The custodian wanted to be seen by staff members as someone who could solve problems rather than someone who always reacted to problems by becoming angry and yelling.

The principal and the custodian engaged in a coaching relationship for the entire year. They met formally about once each month. Informally, they interacted daily as principal and custodian around facility-related issues. These informal interactions helped to build a positive, trusting relationship. Some of the issues addressed in the formal sessions included, "What are options for responding to teachers who want everything NOW?" "How might requests for action from the central office be presented?" "When there are multiple priorities for immediate action, what are some of the factors that need to be considered?" The principal as coach also followed up on previous issues and asked what happened? What worked? What didn't? Have there been any new challenges? Any surprises?

At the end of the year, the custodian said that teachers treated him differently because he had volunteered to be coached. He thought the teachers gave him more respect and knew he was there to learn how to improve, just as the teachers were. He didn't say that his own self-respect had increased in the process, but this was evident in his actions and interactions. Relationships improved. Staff members remarked to the principal that the custodian was more helpful and congenial. Students felt noticeably better about him, too. The custodian accomplished a great deal that year by having the courage to reflect on his behavior, consider alternatives, and chose different actions.

Schoolwide Dyads and Triads

A middle school principal, who was committed to coaching as a way to increase reflection, asked the teachers in his building to form triads for the school year. He knew this could be risky, but he also knew good things could come out of the process. His objective was for these small teams to talk about learning, teaching, students, and education. During workshop week, the staff members chose partners. In the beginning, most groups simply got together and tried to engage in learning conversations. Some just went through the motions of reflective practice. At the end of the school year, the principal asked whether the staff members would be willing to continue these conversations. One staff member declined, and everyone else said they would—as long as one change occurred. They explained that in the beginning, they were unsure and did not know what was going to happen, so they chose to partner with their friends. The next year, they wanted to change reflection partners so there would be a different grade level and different discipline on each triad. The staff members felt they would learn more by having conversations with people from different perspectives rather than with their friends. High praise goes to that staff; learning requires trust. By the end of the year, they were willing to take greater risks to learn more.

Reflection Partners: More Ideas to Consider

Many of the ideas shared in Chapter 3 for reflecting on your own are also well suited for use with partners. For example, reflection on teaching portfolios and professional readings can be greatly enhanced when another person supports the inquiry and learning process. Exchanging teacher narratives or autobiographies offers insight into the thinking and practice of others, which promotes thinking about one's own practice. In the next chapter (5), use of videotapes, book clubs, and teacher dialogues are described as means of reflection in small groups and can also work well for partners. Described below is a menu of ideas for reflecting that may appeal to you and your reflective practice partners.

Dialogue Journals

Dialogue journals, also referred to as interactive journals, are individually written (as described in the journaling section of Chapter 3, pages 52-53) and then shared with another person, who makes inquiries to expand thinking (Keating, 1993). Essentially, this is inquiry through writing instead of through conversation. A principal known by one of the authors of this book engaged in interactive journaling with some of the teachers in his building. Some of the teachers exchanged journals every 2 weeks. Some exchanged them once a month. Two or three days usually passed before journals were returned. Most important, the dialogue was ongoing and could occur outside of face-to-face meetings, which were always difficult to schedule. Equally important, teachers who are more reflective or introverted had time to craft their questions or think about responses. For some, face-to-face interactions are difficult. Refer to the strategies for questioning, responding, and dialogue offered in Chapter 2 (pages 26-33) for specific ideas about comments and questions that prompt reflection.

Structured Dialogue

Pugach and Johnson (1990) conducted a study on the use of a structured dialogue process with general-education classroom teachers to promote reflection on how to more effectively support students with learning and behavior challenges in their classrooms. The goal was to increase the repertoire of effective interventions in the classroom and decrease referrals to special education. The teachers were provided with training about effective interventions and were then coached to engage in self-inquiry about actual classroom challenges involving students with learning and behavior challenges. Teachers were coached through the following four-step process: (a) reframing the problem through clarifying questions; (b) summarizing insights from the reframing process, including the identification of patterns of behavior exhibited by the student and specific variables over which the teacher has control; (c) generating potential actions and predicting the outcomes of each; and (d) developing a plan to evaluate the proposed change. When compared with a control group of teachers, those who participated in the structure dialogue significantly increased their tolerance of student behavior, shifted their attention from student-centered to teacher-centered problem orientation, and increased their confidence in dealing with classroom situations.

Framing Experiences From Practice

Learning from practice, at the preservice or inservice levels, requires learning to think critically about the meaning of real-world experiences. Schall (1995) presented a set of questions used to assist preservice human-services personnel in thinking critically about experiences in the field before presenting them to others for shared reflection: (a) What prompts you to tell the story? (b) What's the moral of your story? What's the specific point you are trying to convey? (c) What is the generalized lesson of the story you or others might abstract; and (d) How could you generalize this lesson and test it? This process has assisted students to focus and discipline their thinking.

> This focusing process allows students to begin to make meaning from the "mess" of their experience at work. The appeal of this approach is its relative simplicity. It does not depend on a master teacher or require only gifted senior level learners. (Schall, 1995, p. 214)

Action Research

One of the most widely recognized and researched ways to systematically reflect on and improve practice is action research. Action research is defined by the Institute for the Study of Inquiry in Education as "a disciplined process of inquiry conducted by and for those taking the action. The primary reason for engaging in action research is to assist the actor in improving and refining his or her actions" (Sagor, 2000, p. 3). Teachers are central in the process of action research. Action research is a structured way to promote reflection on practice and to contribute to the overall development of a professional-learning culture in schools.

Sagor (2000) describes a seven-step, action-research process, "which becomes an endless cycle for the inquiring teacher" (p. 3). The seven steps are: (a) selecting a focus, (b) clarifying theories, (c) identifying research questions, (d) collecting data, (e) analyzing data, (f) reporting results, and (g) taking informed action. This process is similar to other reflection frameworks offered in this book. Important differences, however, are the emphases on formalizing research questions and systematically collecting and analyzing student-performance data.

In recent years, conducting action research on a schoolwide basis has been emphasized (Calhoun, 1994). A primary reason for this is recognition that action research in isolated areas of a school has little or no effect on overall student performance in the school. Action research, therefore, should also be considered as a way to promote learning and reflection at the group or team (Chapter 5) and schoolwide (Chapter 6) levels. Readers interested in learning more about action research can refer to the many comprehensive resources for guidance (see, for example, Glanz, 1994; Glickman, 1995; Lerner, 1997; McLean, 1995; Sagor, 1992, 2000; Stringer, 1996; Taggart & Wilson, 1998).

Weekly Reviews

As teachers begin to work more closely with one another in the design, delivery, and evaluation of instruction for students, they need more time together to plan and reflect. In many schools with diverse student populations, increasing numbers of general educators, special educators, and second-language teachers are co-teaching for some parts of the school day or week, frequently during language arts or math blocks of time. In order to teach together, they must come to know all the students, recognize and use their respective strengths as teachers, and plan for instruction together. In our work with teacher teams, Thursdays consistently emerge as the best day to meet, because the present week can be reviewed, and planning for the next week can begin. At one school, the principal and staff decided to leave every Thursday afternoon open, meaning that no other meetings could be scheduled after school on Thursdays. Early in the school year, meetings of instructional partners usually are consumed by planning units and lessons, determining coteaching roles, and generally getting organized. Over time, the focus shifts to reflecting on individual students who are struggling, work samples from many students, and classroom performance as a whole, which results in regular grouping and regrouping of students. In other words, the emphasis and depth of the reflection evolves as the coteaching relationship and experiences evolve. Regular reflection and dialogue can result in the discovery of new solutions and in ongoing differentiation of instruction to meet varied student needs.

Listening Practice

As educators move toward more collaborative ways of working and learning together, much benefit can be derived from practicing the art of listening through specifically structured activities. We describe here a listening activity developed by a colleague of ours to help people experience and be mindful of what it is like to be heard as well as what it is like to be listened to by someone else for a short period of time. This experience is unique for many people. The activity is organized by forming dyads or triads. In dyads, one person is designated as the listener and the other as the speaker. If triads are used, the three designated roles are listener, speaker, and observer. One person assumes the role of speaker and talks about a particular topic for 3 minutes. During this time, the listener just listens and does not talk. If used, the observer watches both the speaker and listener. At the end of 3 minutes, participants reflect on how their role felt. They then switch roles. Both the speakers and listeners usually comment that both speaking uninterrupted and listening without speaking for 3 minutes is a highly unusual experience. Speakers frequently express appreciation for the time to slow down their thinking. They do not have to worry that a pause in their speaking will result in a loss of their speaking role. Sometimes, speakers are uncomfortable because they are used to being interrupted or to receiving verbal affirmations. Listeners frequently comment on feeling relaxed, because they are not expected to respond immediately. They feel they can listen more deeply because they are not trying to figure out what to say or they are not waiting for air time to get in their perspective. Whatever the response, participants in this type of activity gain insight about the acts of listening and speaking and what a gift they can be, if only for a few minutes. When they don't have to fix the issue or the other people, they can listen more to what is being said within the context of the situation.

Consider carefully the topics for this listening activity. Hot topics can reduce thinking on the part of both listeners and speakers. Emotion begins to take over the process. For example, in one school, there was a lot of controversy about pull-out, special education services. Teachers tended to feel strongly one way or the other. Large-group discussions had not been productive. The listening activity was used in two stages. First, partners took turns listening when the topic was of little consequence (e.g., how they came to be a teacher at that school). Afterward, they processed how that interaction felt and what each was thinking. Second, partners took turns listening to how each another felt about pull-out services and why. Afterward, they processed this listening session as well. Finally, the whole group processed their learning from both sessions and considered both content and process. How did your listening and speaking differ in the different sessions? What accounted for the differences? What could help listening when the topics are more emotionally charged? What did we learn collectively about the issues surrounding pull-out services? Why are those views held?

Observational Learning

For educators to be highly effective, they must become good observers. Taggart and Wilson (1998) explain,

> Observation is a skill that practitioners must possess to develop insights needed to make wise decisions. Observations should be ongoing, systematic, and developed to the point that a focus can be established, notes

taken, and actions explored in a relatively short amount of time with high effectiveness. Inferences and judgments are not components of the observation process, which makes the observation skills difficult for many practitioners. (p. 58)

Written documentation can take the form of a running record, a checklist, or some other observational recording form that is easily used in the flow of instructional routines. Observation provides a way to learn more about students and about teaching by observing peers. Systematic observations with a written documentation of events can serve as the basis for reflection with partners. Facts (description) are shared; interpretation is a collaborative responsibility.

Gitlin (1999) offers an example of four teachers who took turns observing one another teach; these observations were combined with a follow-up dialogue once a month. This approach to reflection and learning was voluntary and teacher directed. The teachers set the agenda for learning through the observations and dialogue. This form of collaboration, as opposed to contrived or mandated collaboration,

Allows questions and priorities of reform to emerge from the teacher dialogue, [and] this approach emphasizes the need for teachers to raise critical concerns about each other's practice, including the taken-for-granted aims, goals, and intentions that inform their work . . . [it] helps to identify tensions between one's teaching philosophy and practice. (Gitlin, 1999, p. 638)

Teachers reported that reflection had become more central in their teaching lives. "Now we talk constantly about what is really important in terms of teaching. . . . This project has [made me] realize that probably one of the best resources of knowledge are the people you work with" (Gitlin, 1999, p. 641).

Getting Started With Reflection Partners

Reflection with a partner is a gift you can give to yourself as well as to a partner. Most of us are driven to learn and improve, and a trusted partner can support our growth. In addition to the benefit of improvements in practice, a relationship is formed that is a valuable resource and support in many aspects of your work life. As you walk down the hallways, into a faculty meeting, or through the work room, you carry with you the assurance that at least one person knows about you, your practice, and your desire to continuously improve. You are not alone. You have extended and deepened your relationship from a more superficial, congenial level of interaction to a more substantial and collaborative interaction with shared commitments to improved practice.

To guide your thinking about moving forward with reflection as partners, we invite you to contemplate the following questions:

- What are my biggest questions about my teaching practice? What do I want to learn more about?

- Why am I drawn to reflecting with a partner or two?

- Who can support and enrich my learning? Who would bring a different perspective that would enrich my learning? Who would be interested in contributing to my growth as an educator?

- What type of environment is conducive to listening, exploring, and thinking?

- How often would I like to, or would it be reasonable to, get together?

- What would make our reflection time a real treat (e.g., coffee and good food)?

- What type of reflection framework or strategy would support our learning together?

The Chapter Reflection: Capturing Your Thoughts form (Figure 4.2) can be used to jot down your thoughts in response to these questions. You may also want to write down the most important learning that occurred for you as you read this chapter.

Some of our greatest insights have emerged from the relative safety of reflection with partners. So, too, have some of our most valued and long-term friendships that provide not only support but also challenges to our thinking and learning processes.

Figure 4.2. Chapter Reflection: Capturing Your Thoughts

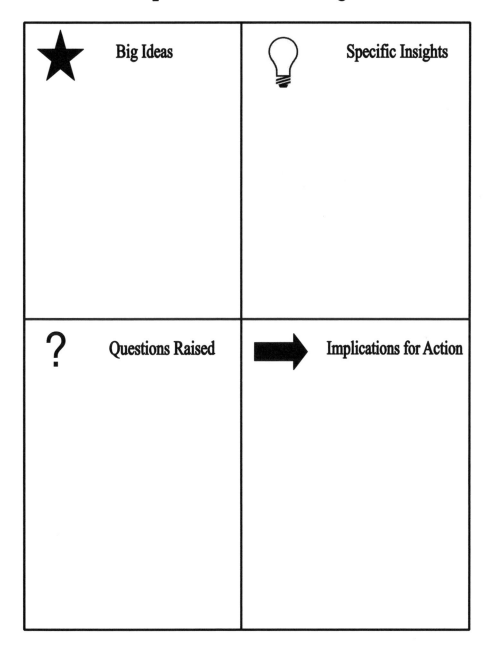

5

Reflection in Small Groups and Teams

Teamwork is often like the weather—everyone talks about it, but often nobody does anything about it. It is seldom achieved by intellectualizing, but is rather the practical application of attitude, common goals, and experience working together. It is a learned art.

—Twyman L. Towery (1995, p. 18)
The Wisdom of Wolves

Clearly, there are a significant number of small groups and teams meeting in schools. Teamwork and collaboration are much-lauded features for today's schools. It is probably not an overstatement to suggest that many educators are on meeting overload. When a new committee is proposed or mandated, a groan is frequently heard from the staff. The questions are, How valuable are these meetings? How much learning is going on? Do the outcomes make a difference in student learning? Does a sense of renewal and recommitment among group members emerge from the meetings? Which meetings are real? meaning that there is an important purpose for meeting and that productive outcomes emerge. And which meetings are pretend? meaning that nothing of much value comes of the time and energy expended. Meeting in groups and teams is commonplace, but reflection and learning in these situations are not.

Face-to-face meeting time is perhaps the most valuable learning resource in schools. We argue that the vast majority of this time should be spent reflecting and learning together in ways that positively impact student learning. Given the increasing diversity, complexity, and pace in the field of education, learning together about being effective in "the swamp" of practice (see Schon, 1987, Chapter 1, p. 4) is a necessity. "Reflective practice is vital for the swamp. It enables people to be present and it helps them and their organizations make meaning from what are generally complex, multidimensional experiences" (Schall, 1995, p. 208). External knowledge and resources go only so far to support educational practice. Groups of educators frequently have tasks that are somewhat open-ended and require shared inquiry in order to come up with new understandings, interventions, and plans. Educators must "work together to construct knowledge rather than to discover objective truths" (Cranton, 1996, p. 27) as a primary way of advancing practice. "Teamwork is itself both a process and a principle [of adult learning]" (Vella, 1994, p. 19).

In a recent study that compared teamed and nonteamed middle school teachers, Pounder (1999) found that teamed teachers (i.e., those whose jobs had a shared work-group emphasis) reported significantly higher levels of knowledge about students, skill variety in their work, helpfulness and effectiveness within their work group, teaching efficacy, professional commitment, and overall satisfaction and growth. Survey data from students in both schools indicated that students in the teamed school were more satisfied with their relationships with other students and with safety and student discipline. They were less satisfied, however, with the nature and amount of schoolwork. In other words, they were more likely to be held accountable to high and shared expectations by the group of teamed teachers. Reflecting on the overall findings from the study, the author suggested that "the most encouraging of these results may be the increased knowledge that teamed teachers seem to gain about students" (Pounder, 1999, p. 338). The design of effective instruction begins with understanding the abilities, interests, challenges, and learning strengths experienced by individual students. Learning together in teams or small groups, educators can increase their understanding of students as well as their practice.

The journey toward reflection and learning in groups and teams is not easily traveled. "Teamwork cannot be taken for granted. . . . Teams present new problems in the learning situation [and] people must learn how to work together efficiently" (Vella, 1994, p. 20). One of the greatest challenges when reflecting in groups and teams is the establishment of trust. Contrary to the adage claiming safety in numbers, Osterman and Kottkamp (1993) remind us,

> Reflective practice in a group setting is a high risk process. . . . In most organizations, problems are viewed as a sign of weakness . . . to break this conspiracy of silence requires new organizational norms. To engage in the reflective process, individuals need to believe that discussions of problems will not be interpreted as incompetence or weakness. (pp. 44-55)

Despite the inherent risks and challenges involved in expanding reflective practice to groups or teams, there are good reasons to venture forth into this domain. Recall from Chapter 1 (see page 15), the potential gains that can be realized at the group or team level of the reflective practice spiral (Figure 5.1). More resources (e.g., experience, knowledge, energy) are brought to the process of reflecting on

Figure 5.1. The Reflective Practice Spiral With Small-Group Level Highlighted

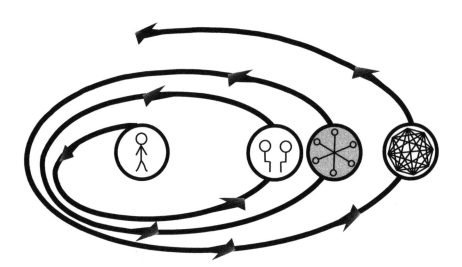

practice and implementing new ideas. Reflection as small groups and teams also increases collegiality and a sense of potential to accomplish significant improvements. In general, as the number of people involved in reflective practice increases, so, too, does the potential to improve schools and the need to carefully consider how to promote effective interactions among group and team members. Design is critical. As a teacher, think about the difference between working with a small group of 5 students compared with a group of 25 students. Productive learning does not just happen in groups of children or in groups of adults. There is a much greater need for design, orchestration, and ongoing reflection-in-action. An underlying principle in group design is to maximize participation and commitment so that the collective resources of the group are best used to improve learning for students.

In this chapter, we expand the how-to reflective-practice information, which was presented in previous chapters for individuals and small groups, to address how to promote reflective practice within groups and teams. Again, we offer considerations, examples, ideas, and suggestions for getting started with reflective practice in small groups.

Special Considerations for Reflection in Small Groups and Teams

Many educators have become skeptical and resistant about being in small groups, teams, and especially committees. Honestly, many have good reasons for their views. Through experience, they have learned that working in groups is often risky, frustrating, and unproductive. In short, it has been a waste of their time. Learning in groups has been a rare exception to the rule. The likelihood of negative prior experiences makes it both more difficult and more important that efforts to promote reflection and learning in groups be carefully designed and facilitated. A period of unlearning precedes new learning. In other words, reluctant members must move through the stage of "prove that it is going to be different this time" before they will choose to expend energy and risk participation in group reflection and learning.

In this section, special considerations for designing reflective practices in small groups, teams, or committees are identified and discussed. Our intent is to address the question, "What is known about promoting interactions among educators that results in learning and effectiveness in the context of a small group?" We offer a short-course response. Many excellent resources respond to this question in a more comprehensive manner (see, for example, Garmston & Wellman, 1999; Hare, 1994; Johnson & Johnson, 1999; Thousand & Villa, 2000). The purpose of engaging in reflective practice is the primary consideration and has been addressed previously in Chapter 2 (pp. 33-37), with the main point being that educators are more likely to engage in reflective group work if the purpose has meaning for their immediate practice and is likely to make a difference for students. Described below are considerations related to the nature of group development, group participants and their roles, and effective group processes for supporting reflection and learning. Also addressed are considerations related to the precious resource of time. As you review this information, keep in mind that there are no absolutes for designing group learning. There are only considerations that must be continuously reflected on to determine application and modification in specific local contexts.

What Can Be Expected in Terms of Group Development Over Time?

One significant influence on reflection and learning in groups is the nature of how groups develop over time. In the classic work of Tuckman (1965), four phases of group development are identified: forming, storming, norming, and performing (Figure 5.2). In the *forming* phase, groups experience relative niceness. Members are introduced to one another and to the task at hand. They typically interact somewhat cautiously if not superficially. This is a period of checking out one another. How do individuals relate to the group's purpose and members? How safe is it here? What is the potential for accomplishing something meaningful? Are there things I can learn from this experience? Do I have something to contribute?

As group members come to know one another and begin to figure out their task, a period of *storming* ensues. How does the specific work of the group become defined? What are the best ways to proceed? What is important to each group member? How are different perspectives heard and responded to? What are the

Figure 5.2. Diagram of Tuckman's (1965) Phases of Group Development

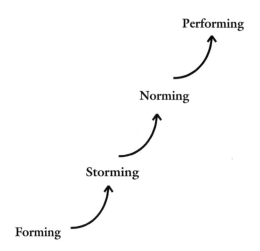

sources of conflict, and which ones need to be addressed? Who participates, who doesn't, and why? What can be done about it? It is during this storming phase of group development that many groups fall apart. Even if group members continue to attend meetings, they may psychologically disengage or, worse, choose to behave in counterproductive ways. To move forward requires that group members learn how to interact with one another respectfully and how to engage in effective group processes. Sometimes, it is necessary for either an external or internal facilitator or a combined facilitation team to support groups, especially in the early stages of norming and storming.

If the group successfully navigates the storming phase, they move into a period of relative calm and clarity referred to as *norming*. This is when members have clarified their task and have figured out how it will be addressed by the group. Members know one another better. Individual strengths (e.g., organization, humor, focus, connections) and preferences (e.g., room arrangements, agenda sequence, food) are sorted out and used to the advantage of the group. Most important, learning has occurred in the area of group process that results in greater efficiency. Groups and teams experience a learning curve just as individuals do. Efficiency and higher performance come after learning and practicing new skills, processes, and ways of thinking. It is at this point that groups reach the *performing* phase.

Without an appreciation of the phases of group development, group members can interpret storming as a sign of ineffectiveness instead of as an inevitable part of the messiness of becoming a functioning group. Viewed in a more personal context, most of us can relate well to this developmental process. Recall times in your life when you and another person (e.g., sibling, roommate, stepparent, partner) took up shared residence. Wasn't there a period of adjustment? This involved learning about each other in a new way, observing different ways of doing things (e.g., laundry, dishes), deciding on how to manage shared responsibilities (e.g., bills and chores), and finally, figuring out how to live together. Learning how to work well in groups involves coming to know one another as individuals as you join together around shared goals.

Who Participates and What Are Their Roles?

Several major considerations are related to who participates in learning groups and their roles in the group process: group size, group composition, and group-member roles. Each of these is addressed below.

Group Size

Recently, we sat in on grade-level team meetings in an elementary school. The third-grade team had 7 people in attendance; the fourth-grade team had 12. Considering just the variable of size, which group was more likely to have participation and why? An optimal group size for working and learning together is considered to be 4 to 6 people (Johnson & Johnson, 1999). This size offers varied perspectives and skills while still allowing, if not subtly requiring, participation by all members. Somewhat larger groups of educators frequently are necessary in schools. Groups of 8 to 10 can still function well (Hare, 1994; Thousand & Villa, 2000) if relationships are developed and processes are well designed and implemented.

Beyond the general parameter of number, group size is influenced by many factors. Who has a relevant perspective on the issue? Who would benefit from participation? Who will be expected to follow through with decisions made by the group? How big is the meeting area? Who is available at a common meeting time? What is the nature of the task? For short-term and specific tasks, groups of 2 or 3 may be preferable. For more complicated tasks, a larger number may be involved. When groups are large, individual participation can be increased by breaking into smaller groups for specific interactions. For example, in a group of 15, participants might be asked to form subgroups of 3 to 5 people to reflect on a specific issue and then share their subgroup's reflections with the entire group.

In general, groups need to be big enough to offer a variety of perspectives and to have sufficient resources for learning and work to be accomplished. They should be small enough to promote trust and participation among members.

Group Composition

One overarching consideration related to who participates is the need to *get all the voices in the room,* including those who have different viewpoints. Without them in the room, plans are doomed, either due to sabotage or because the missing voices were needed to construct a workable plan. Another consideration in determining group composition is the *heterogeneity-versus-homogeneity dimension* related to characteristics such as gender, age, race, amount, and type of experience, and disciplinary or content-area background. Heterogeneity in groups has the potential to enhance learning, given the enriched pool of information, perspectives, and skills. Teams formed to explore integrated service models, for example, should involve general educators, special educators, and second-language teachers. Groups formed to determine space use in a school should include teachers from across content areas and grade levels. Committees formed to provide leadership and oversight for staff development should include teachers and administrators representing the many varied school and district constituents. Another reason to promote heterogeneous group composition is to intentionally foster connections among people who rarely see one another. Recall the web of relationships (Figure 1.3 on page 18) described in Chapter 1 and the benefits that can be realized for students, staff, and improvement initiatives when a rich network of quality relationships extends throughout a school.

Having just promoted the value of heterogeneity, we will point out that it is also true that relatively homogeneous-group composition is at times appropriate and productive. For example, early in the process of becoming more reflective, educators may feel more comfortable examining their practices with colleagues whom they know well and who have similar experiences and perspectives. This allows skill development and practice in a relatively safe environment. Reviewing science curricula for possible adoption reasonably falls to science teachers. A team of teachers who work with third-grade students decide effectively on strategies to prepare third-grade students for the annual statewide tests for third graders. The degree of homogeneity and heterogeneity within a group will depend, in part, on the purpose of the group.

Another important consideration for group composition is the *voluntary-versus-mandated dimension*. The value of voluntary or even self-organized learning groups is readily understood. Initiation, interest, and self-direction are high motivators for learning, ownership, and commitment. Mandated assignments, by their very nature, communicate a power-over relationship and serve as a reminder of the hierarchical organization of schools. This dynamic can be interpreted as a lack of respect and professionalism and result in unprofessional behavior. At "prison" (i.e., mandated) inservices, for example, you can count on about a third of the participants being mad when they walk into the room. Sometimes, being invited or asked to participate results in participation but lessens the negative effects of mandates. As much as possible, teachers should be partners in the process of determining group composition. "Respecting people as subjects, try to have people choose their own teams as often as possible, especially when the learning task is complex and difficult" (Vella, 1994, p. 18). Frequently, participation of specific individuals may require that they be requested or invited. Sometimes, circumstances require mandated participation. When this is the case, recognize that the only type of participation that can be mandated is physical presence. Genuine engagement of the heart and mind comes only from the inside out. With a mandate in place, it is even more important to intentionally design the group process to promote active engagement.

One final consideration related to group composition is the *existing-versus-reconfigured dimension*. Depending on the purpose of the group and the people who should be involved, new groups may be convened, existing groups may be used, or existing groups may be reconfigured. After groups have been together for awhile, two threats to effectiveness can emerge: Groupthink (Fullan & Stiegelbauer, 1991) and group assumptions. Groupthink is evident when there has ceased to be any inquiry or challenge. The group falls into predictable and unproductive patterns of engaging in and responding to tasks in the same way. Nothing new is going on—no new learning, no new generation of ideas, no alternative perspectives. Group assumptions are the unspoken expectations about how people behave. Group members come to be viewed as demonstrating predictable and sometimes unproductive patterns of participation. Others come to expect such behavior. Prior attempts to adjust these patterns may have been punished, ignored, or otherwise unsuccessful. The result is that groups become stuck, and it is time for a change. New people or new combinations of people can have the effect of unfreezing thinking, routines, and expectations. An opportunity is created to set new expectations, to consider new roles and patterns of participation, to establish a culture of learning and inquiry before unproductive norms take hold and the refreezing process sets in. New people bring new potential and energy that can be put to good use with an intentional design to support learning and reflection.

Group-Member Roles

Sharing responsibility for group learning and working together enhances effectiveness. The most important role for which all group members are responsible is engaged participant (Garmston & Wellman, 1997, 1999). In the absence of engaged participation by group members, nothing much is accomplished. "In strong groups, engaged participants monitor their personal adherence to meeting standards . . . [and also] monitor the group's adherence to standards" (p. 82). Other roles that are frequently assigned and sometimes rotated among group members include facilitator, recorder, timekeeper, and observer. Some group members may also have role authority or knowledge authority (Garmston & Wellman, 1997, 1999). Examples of someone with role authority are a principal who is a group member with a teacher from her building, and a curriculum director who participates as a member of a group of content-area lead teachers. By nature of their positions, the principal and curriculum director have authority over other members. A group member with knowledge authority has a high level of expertise about the content focus of the group. A group member with role authority has a high level of knowledge about policies, mandates, budgets, and other structures that may affect the group's work and decisions. General responsibilities for group-member roles are listed in Table 5.1, drawing from the work of several authors (e.g., Garmston &

TABLE 5.1 Group-Member Roles

Participant

- Listens well
- Contributes own perspective
- Assists process, movement of group
- Demonstrates awareness of self and others
- Seeks information, clarification, and other perspectives
- Monitors own and group behavior

Facilitator

- Clarifies purpose, task, process
- Guides process to assure participation
- Monitors and adjusts process as needed
- Remains neutral about topic and outcome
- Solicits summary and clarification about follow-up

Recorder

- Listens well, stays alert, and remains neutral
- Records main ideas using participants' words
- Seeks clarification and correction
- Summarizes and checks for accuracy

Timekeeper

- Monitors use of time
- Alerts group about time limits

Observer

- Formally or informally monitors group process and interaction
- Provides feedback about observations for group reflection

Content authority

- Contributes knowledge and experienced perspective about content or task focus

Role authority

- Provides oversight, support, and coordination regarding resources, decisions, and follow-through

SOURCE: Adapted from Garmston, R., & Wellman, B. (1999); Thousand, J. S., & Villa, R. (2000); York-Barr, J., Kronberg, R., & Doyle, M. B. (1995).

Wellman, 1997, 1999; Thousand & Villa, 2000; York-Barr, Kronberg, & Doyle, 1996).

The role of facilitator requires special consideration in the design of reflection and learning in groups and teams. Osterman and Kottkamp (1993) explain that frequently "reflective practice requires a facilitator, someone who helps to begin the process and assumes responsibility for ensuring the participants' safety" (p. 46). Three primary goals of the facilitator are facilitating task accomplishment, the development of group skills and processes, and the overall development of a group (Garmston & Wellman, 1999). It is often the case that individuals who are assigned to or who assume responsibility for running groups come to that position without a full understanding of the significance of this assignment and how to effectively guide the learning and working process of the group. It is not unusual for assigned facilitators to view their role as moving through an agenda, sometimes with expedience.

Killion and Simmons (1992) make important distinctions between a training perspective on working with groups and a facilitation perspective. In a training session, trainers are responsible for providing specific information to participants and for focusing on the development of predetermined skills and outcomes. It is the trainer's job to cover certain material and to teach participants. In contrast, in a facilitated group session, it is the job of the facilitator to guide the group through processes to discover its own specific outcomes. The task of the group is usually more open and requires that group members listen, learn, and figure things out together. The facilitator makes easier the work of the group. Training is an outside-in process. Facilitation is an inside-out process.

So what makes a good facilitator? First and foremost, effective factilitators must be trusted by members of the group. They must also trust the group and have confidence in the ability of its members to come up with their own best learning and applications when engaged in a meaningful and effective process. Recognizing that underlying beliefs and values influence behaviors, Osterman and Kottkamp (1993) describe beliefs that serve as the foundation for an effective facilitator:

> To serve as an effective facilitator, actions have to be grounded in a certain set of beliefs, beliefs that reflect a deep commitment to the potential for human change and development. These beliefs about professional development constitute a "credo for reflective practice."

- Everyone needs professional growth opportunities
- All professionals want to improve
- All professionals can learn
- All professionals are capable of assuming responsibility for their own professional growth and development
- People need and want information about their performance
- Collaboration enriches professional development

True feelings are conveyed in very subtle ways that are difficult to disguise. Unless the facilitator has a deep commitment to these beliefs about professional development—or at least can suspend doubt—she or he will be unable to disguise real feelings. The facilitator has to be a person who not only espouses this educational philosophy but who can convince others through deeds that he or she can be trusted to fulfill the obligation. (pp. 46-47)

Osterman and Kottkamp also present a want ad for a reflective practice facilitator that eloquently captures the characteristics of an individual well suited for that role (Figure 5.3).

Given the primary importance of trust between the facilitator and group members as well as among group members themselves, "The facilitator must be skilled at developing an environment in which the participants feel comfortable enough to contribute actively (safety) and an environment in which they have the opportunity to participate (equity)" (Osterman & Kottkamp, 1993, p. 63). How can you get a read on the degree of safety felt by group participants? The energy level is a good indicator (Vella, 1994). Vella (1994) refers to the *fatal plop* that endangers the safety in a group.

The fatal plop [is] when an adult learner says something in a group, only to have the words hit the floor with a resounding "plop," without affirmation, without even recognition that she has spoken, with the teacher proceeding as if nothing had been said—[this] is a great way to destroy safety. (p. 8)

She goes on to explain that the fatal plop destroys safety not only for the one person but also for everyone in the group. As an individual, then, a facilitator must demonstrate capacities for promoting trust (described previously in Chapter 2, pages 23-26): Be present, be open, listen, seek understanding, assume mutuality, and honor the person.

Effective facilitators are always thinking about their thinking (i.e., metacognition) in the process of facilitating the group process. This is a form of reflection-in-action, one of the most sophisticated ways of reflecting. Garmston and Wellman (1999, p. 90) identify five metacognitive capabilities that promote this capacity:

- To know one's intention and choose congruent behaviors

- To set aside unproductive patterns of listening, responding, and inquiry

- To know when to assert and when to integrate

- To know and support the group's purposes, topics, processes, and development

- To emotionally disassociate from events in order to make strategic decisions about process

Figure 5.3. Reflective Practice Facilitator Position Description

---

Position Available:
Facilitator for Reflective Practice
WANTED

A person who is inherently curious; someone who doesn't have all the answers and isn't afraid to admit it; someone who is confident enough in his or her ability to accept challenges in a nondefensive manner; someone who is secure enough to make his or her thinking public and therefore subject to discussion; someone who is a good listener; someone who likes other people and trusts them to make the right decisions if given the opportunity; someone who is able to see things from another's perspective and is sensitive to the needs and feelings of others; someone who is able to relax and lean back and let others assume the responsibility of their own learning. Some experience desirable but not as important as the ability to learn from mistakes.

SOURCE: Osterman, K. F., & Kottkamp, R. B. (1993). *Reflective Practice for Educators: Improving Schooling Through Professional Development,* p. 64. Copyright © 1993. Reprinted by permission of Corwin Press, Inc.

Effective facilitators must also be skilled at promoting thinking through questioning and responding. They must be particularly adept at facilitating dialogue, given its powerful effect on adult learning (Vella, 1994). Thinking, questioning, responding, and engaging in dialogue are capacities for not only the facilitator but also group members (see Chapter 2, pages 26-33 for more information about these capacities). Finally, an effective facilitator guides groups through constructive dialogue, viewing issues and events from different perspectives, generating ideas, solving problems, managing and learning from conflict, and making decisions.

Who facilitates? In most schools, a member of the group or some other person from within the school or district facilitates formally or informally. Sometimes, an external person is used. Advantages and disadvantages of use of internal and external facilitators are listed in Table 5.2. Internal facilitators are usually more readily available, and they bring a better understanding of the context. As a facilitator, however, they may have difficulty remaining neutral, and they are not free to be a group participant. External facilitators bring a more objective perspective and are likely to bring more expertise as a facilitator. They offer the distinct advantage of allowing insiders to participate fully as group members. They can also be costly and less convenient in terms of scheduling and communication.

Individuals with role and knowledge authority also present particular advantages and disadvantages as facilitators. Individuals with role authority may have the advantage of information regarding budget, policy, and a more comprehensive systems perspective. They have the potential disadvantage of confusing their role of facilitator and their role of boss. Another disadvantage is that group members may

TABLE 5.2 Potential Advantages and Disadvantages of Internal and External Facilitators

	Potential Advantages	*Potential Disadvantages*
Internal facilitator	Knowledge of context (e.g., issues, resources, individuals)	Bias given knowledge of context
	Opportunity to build or expand relationships internally	Personal or professional interest in the outcome
	Aware of group outcomes and needs	Role confusion for facilitator and participants
	Builds internal capacity for facilitation	Potential for less expertise related to facilitation than external person (e.g., consultant)
		Cannot participate as a participant (i.e., voice is lost from the group)
External facilitator	Little knowledge of context, increased ability to remain neutral	Little knowledge of context, reduced ability to see all aspects of issues
	Expertise in facilitation and group-process skills	Must establish credibility with group
		May be less convenient (e.g., scheduling, time, communication)
		May be expensive

be concerned about repercussions. This can diminish participation by group members. Individuals with knowledge authority can bring valuable information and perspective to a group, but they may also have difficulty moving outside of their expert role to facilitate new learning that meets the needs and goals of the group. This can inhibit the generation of knowledge and expertise from within the group. The knowledge authority as facilitator can easily create confusion between the facilitator role and the role of expert.

When deciding who might facilitate group learning and process, the purpose of the group and characteristics of the individual are important considerations. Perhaps the most important consideration is whom the group will allow to serve as facilitator. Who can stay focused on the process and participation without getting stuck in the content or dynamics? A trusting relationship between facilitator and group participants has to exist or emerge (Osterman & Kottkamp, 1993; Vella, 1994). We often encourage pairs of teachers to facilitate. When facilitation is shared, one person can observe the process and participants while the other assumes responsibility to guide the process. Teamed facilitators can take turns in each role. This also provides the opportunity for shared reflection on the group's process after the group adjourns: What worked? What did not work? Why?

When facilitators emerge within groups, they must be clear about when they are in the role of facilitator and when they are in the role of participant. This helps group members understand the difference and minimizes the likelihood of group members feeling manipulated because someone leads the process who has a vested interest in the actions and outcomes. When it is necessary or appropriate to be in the role of participant, facilitators formally step out of that role. They inform the group that they are taking off the hat of facilitator temporarily, to contribute their perspective as a group member. They then share their own perspective and provide the opportunity for others to interact with them while still in the group-member role. They can then return to the role of facilitating the group's process. It is difficult to facilitate well when one is also a group member, and it requires a high level of awareness about one's thinking, assumptions, biases, desires, and roles. After groups move to a point of learning and working together well, a formal facilitator role becomes less important or can be easily rotated among group members.

What Structures and Processes
Support Group Reflection and Learning?

As suggested previously, it cannot be assumed that individuals know how to interact effectively in the context of a group (Will, 1997), even when they reflect well as individuals. Groups are a different context and require an expanded repertoire of skills and processes. Specific group structures and processes assist in creating the conditions that promote participation, thinking, learning, and working together. Especially in a group's early work, careful attention to design and facilitation is important. In a major study of different kinds of work groups and what makes them effective, Hackman (1991) identified a significant finding referred to as *self-fueling spirals,* meaning that over time, the rich get richer and the poor get poorer. If groups got off to a good start, they tended to perform better over time. Conversely, if they did not get off to a good start, they tended to perform poorly over time. How, then, can the likelihood of a good start be maximized?

There must be an intentional design to create a safe and productive learning environment. In considering safety, however, recall from the previous chapter that learning, particularly learning that involves frame breaking, necessarily involves periods of discomfort. "Safety does not obviate the natural challenge of learning new concepts, skills, or attitudes. Safety does not take away from the hard work of learning" (Vella, 1994, p. 6). Considerations related to the structures and processes for learning in groups are presented below in the following sequence: planning for groups, opening the group process, engaging in the core agenda, closing the group process.

Planning for Groups

Planning for groups is a form of reflection-for-action. While keeping in mind the desired outcomes for the group session, designers need to think through how to bring the group to a common focus, to promote a safe and participatory climate, and to facilitate effective interactions. In new groups, large groups, and groups facing known challenges (e.g., conflicted issues, difficult interpersonal dynamics), a tighter process may be needed. Adherence to an agenda can decrease the likelihood of unproductive interactions. However, an agenda that is too tight or a process that is too controlled can result in diminished or superficial participation. Some groups, especially those that are self-organized, rarely need a formal agenda or carefully sequenced process. The group's purpose and participants influence the specific design for group interaction significantly. The examples provided later in this chapter show different structures that align with the characteristics of different groups. Magestro and Stanford-Blair (2000) outline a planning template for staff development that occurs in groups. A slightly modified version of their template is outlined here:

- *Identify the purpose and objectives* of the meeting: What do you want participants to learn and be able to do as a result of this activity?

- *Select the resources* you plan to use as a basis for the activity. Include both content resources (e.g., journal articles, books, videos, inquiry kits) and process resources (e.g., overhead transparencies, flip charts).

- *Prepare an agenda* that fits the time frame available. Include an activator (i.e., an activity to elicit prior knowledge, beliefs, or attitudes), brief input (usually information from the content resources), interaction (opportunities for participants to reflect on, engage with, and respond to the input), and summarizer (individual or group activity that brings attention to important aspects of the learning and that specifies personal commitments for follow-up).

- *Specify revisit or follow-up activities,* such as peer planning or coaching.

Consider carefully the location, time, physical-space arrangement, and refreshments. Convenience, comfort, and quality are three, sometimes competing, dimensions to consider. The most convenient location is usually at the school site. If the meeting location is off-site, there are the deterrents of travel time and directions. Some people will choose not to attend. Meeting off-site, however, offers some quality advantages, such as the potential for being served good food and drink (e.g., at a coffee shop), meeting in a room designed for adult learning (e.g., seated comfortably in adult-size chairs around tables as opposed to meeting in child-size desks and chairs), and settling in to an environment that supports thinking (e.g., a pleasant room with windows and a peaceful view). Most important, meeting off-site greatly diminishes the inevitable distractions (e.g., people coming and going, bells, unexpected student issues). Early in a group formation and learning process, it can be very advantageous to arrange for off-site meetings and allocate larger periods of time so that participants are comfortable, not distracted, and have enough time to settle in to a reflective mode.

Finding common times to meet is a major challenge. Specific ideas and strategies are offered later in this chapter on pages 99-103. In addition, one of the practice examples for reflecting in groups is a site-based, task-force process focused on scheduling time for teams to meet. Before and after school are usually the most convenient times but can pose quality constraints. Before school, participants can be distracted, given the impending start of the instructional day. After school, participants can be either drained or wound up. Usually, periods in the middle of the day have both problems. Release time provides the best quality advantage, as long as students do not incur instructional disadvantages. Depending on the nature of the task, half-day meeting blocks are usually effective and can sometimes be arranged through internal coverage from midday forward. When time to meet is anywhere around the instructional day, the structure of the meeting must include an activity that assists in the transition from the fast-paced instructional day to more reflective learning time.

The physical arrangement of the meeting area also affects reflection and learning. In general, participants should be arranged in a circle so they can easily see one another. The reason for this is captured in the words of a Sioux elder (Lame Deer & Erdoes, 1994), presented in Figure 5.4. Circles diminish a power orientation. The desired interaction is among members of the group, not between the group and a facilitator, for example. Chairs should be made for adults and comfortable. If the group is to use paper or other materials, participants can be comfortably arranged around tables that are large enough to hold the materials and allow room to work but are small enough for everyone to feel connected to one another (Vella, 1994). If there is to be a considerable amount of presenting, active facilitation, or public recording, a U-shaped arrangement can work well. The key design features are comfort, openness, and participants facing one another.

Finally, planning for refreshments, even if just cool, fresh water or hot water with tea and coffee bags, indicates a degree of caring for the physical needs of participants. Ongoing groups frequently rotate responsibilities for refreshments. Sometimes, this responsibility takes care of itself when groups decide to meet at conveniently located restaurants.

Opening the Group Process

The way in which a group or meeting begins communicates to the participants the degree of safety, respect, preparation, and perceived importance of the time planned together. Participants should be welcomed as they arrive, greeted by name if possible, and invited to help themselves to refreshments. This begins the process of acknowledgement, communicates caring, and assists with the psychological transition from where they were to where they are—soon to be engaged partici-

Figure 5.4. Sioux Elder's Explanation of the Symbolism of Circles

A reading from John
Lame Deer, a Sioux Elder

We Indians live in a world of symbols and images where the spiritual and commonplace are one. To you symbols are just words, spoken or written in a book. To us they are a part of nature, part of ourselves—the earth, the sun, the wind, and the rain, stones, trees, animals, even little insects like ants and grasshoppers. We try to understand them not with the head but with the heart, and we need no more than a hint to give us the meaning. . . . To our way of thinking the Indians' symbol is the circle, the hoop. Nature wants things to be round. The bodies of human beings and animals have no corners. With us the circle stands for the togetherness of people who sit with one another around the campfire, relatives and friends united in peace while the pipe passes from hand to hand. The camp in which every tipi had its place was also a ring. The tipi was a ring in which people sat in a circle and all families in the village were in turn circles within a larger circle, part of the larger hoop which was the seven campfires of the Sioux, representing one nation. The nation was only part of the universe, in itself circular and made of earth, which is round, of the sun, which is round, of the stars, which are round. The moon, the horizon, the rainbow—circles within circles, with no beginning and no end.

SOURCE: Lame Deer, J., & Erdoes, R. (1994), p. 108, 110-111.

pants in a group learning process. Here are some other guidelines for initiating the group:

Introductions Make sure participants get to know one another by name, position, and relationship to the group (i.e., why are they participants). Use nametags if necessary or write names on in order chart paper.

Overview and Review Reference an agenda (either posted or on handouts) and introduce the purpose of the meeting—both the BIG purpose (i.e., the long-term goal of the group) and the more focused purpose of the current meeting. Provide an overview of the activities, time frames, process, and desired outcomes. Ask for input and solicit questions. Assign group roles as appropriate. In subsequent meetings, review the process and outcomes of the previous meeting. These activities clarify purpose and orient the group to the present.

Relationship-Building Activities Use relationship-building activities, especially early in formation of the group. These activities should be safe but personal (Will, 1997). For example, ask participants to share a little-known fact about themselves, describe a favorite family ritual, and inform the group about where they were born, or find out who travels the farthest to get to school every day. This provides an opportunity for participants to practice disclosure in a safe way (they determine what to share and what not to share) and offers another way to know each person in the group, which assists with remembering names. In a recent meeting, one teacher shared that as a young child, she tried to teach her pet fish to walk. Another young teacher shared that just a few years ago, he was in the best physical shape ever and experienced a stroke. Each of these disclosures expands the understanding and connections among group members. Through stories of humorous events or personal challenges, individuals become connected in another way besides around work. This strengthens the relationships. Building relationships promotes commitment to group participants, processes, and purpose. This is especially helpful as groups move into more difficult areas of inquiry and sharing. One way to keep this type of activity going is for pairs of participants to rotate responsibility for leading an icebreaking activity at the beginning of each session.

Group Norms and Expectations Paying attention to norms and expectations at every session serves as a reminder of behaviors and dispositions that facilitate learning and working together. We frequently begin group sessions with the verbal or visual reminder that "we are all in the same room, but not in the same place" (anonymous as quoted by Garmston & Wellman, 1997, p. 29). This serves to acknowledge differences among individuals and to support the emergence of varied perspectives. Norms and expectations can be offered or generated or a combination of both. They should be posted in clear view. For starters, you could offer the personal capacities for reflection described in Chapter 2 (pages 23-33). We suggest the seven norms of collaborative work generated by Bill Baker and formally articulated in the work of Garmston and Wellman (1997; 1999). "When the seven norms of collaborative work become an established part of group life and group work, cohesion, energy, and commitment to shared work and to the group increase dramatically" (Garmston & Wellman, 1999, p. 37). Figure 5.5 shows these norms along with a visual reminder to consider dialogue, discussion, and suspension as tools for individual and group use. This depiction, which we call the *tabletop norms,* has been formatted to fit in a 5-by-7 inch self-standing plastic frame. Presented in this way, the norms can be placed on tables within the group. To be effective, groups must regularly revisit the norms and commit to practice. One way to do this

Figure 5.5. Tabletop Norms

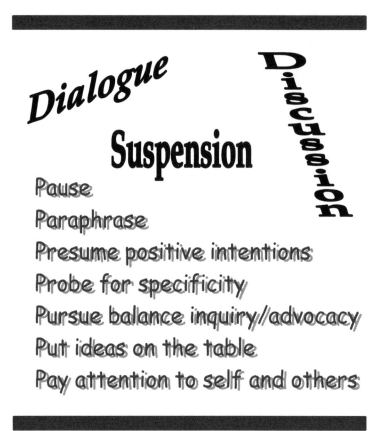

SOURCE: Adapted with permission from Garmston, R., & Wellman, B. (1999). *The Adaptive School: A Sourcebook for Developing Collaborative Groups.* Norwood, MA: Christopher Gordon Publishers.

is for individuals or an entire group to identify at the start of each meeting a norm on which they would like to focus for that meeting.

Engaging in the Core Agenda

Developing effective ways of reflecting and learning together as a group requires consciousness about the process in addition to the tasks and outcomes. Engaging in the core part of a meeting requires reflection-in-action. As the group begins to move through the core agenda, participation is monitored. Over time, all participants assist in this monitoring process. Initially the group members who assume the roles of facilitator, recorder, timekeeper, and observer may be more active. Adhering to the seven norms of collaborative work (Figure 5.5) or another agreed-on framework for interaction enhances effectiveness. Moving forward can require redirecting the group to the present focus, checking in to see if more or less time is needed for specific interactions, creating space to share for individuals who hesitate or refrain from sharing, requesting clarification or a summary of ideas, or breaking down into pairs or small groups to promote greater participation. When groups are in the early phases of learning effective processes, explicit guidance may be required about how to dialogue, diagnose problems, generate ideas, manage conflict, make decisions, and plan for the future. For example, stating when the group is in dialogue (understanding), as opposed to discussion (deciding), increases awareness about ways participants might think and respond. If shifting the conversation to discussion results in high degrees of conflict and strong advocacy, it may be necessary to intentionally shift the process back to dialogue. Sometimes, to increase participation in a larger group, it may be necessary to break down into smaller groups for part of the process.

Closing the Group Process

Bringing a group session to a close takes the form of reflection-on-action. The main functions are summarizing the content and debriefing the process. "People need to feel that the work of the group is meaningful if they are to take such activities seriously in the future" (Will, 1997, p. 37). Summarizing the content involves restating the session purpose, highlighting main insights or outcomes, specifying follow-up, and projecting the purpose and activities for future sessions. Debriefing the process involves reflection on how effectively the group learned and worked together.

We offer three options for group reflection and closure: posing general questions, using reflection frameworks, and responding to group-process checklists. Each of these options can take the form of whole-group, or small-group then whole-group, or individual then whole-group processing. General questions might include a focus on the content, for example, "What were the most significant insights or outcomes of today's gathering?" and a focus on process, for example, "What were strengths in terms of our overall group process and what might be some things to work on next time?"

A variety of reflection frameworks that can target both content and process are shown in Figure 5.6. Used most effectively, they would first involve asking participants to spend a few moments responding on their own or with a partner and then sharing with the whole group. A fun way to share with the whole group is using the crumple 'n' toss activity. This involves everyone writing their responses to the reflection questions. Then, when everyone is finished writing, they crumple their papers and toss them to a central location (we have used a children's basketball hoop). Each participant then randomly takes one crumpled piece of paper, uncrumples it, and takes a turn reading the response to the group. Particularly in large groups, this results in anonymous but comprehensive sharing of group members' perspectives.

Figure 5.6. Sample of Closing Reflection Worksheets

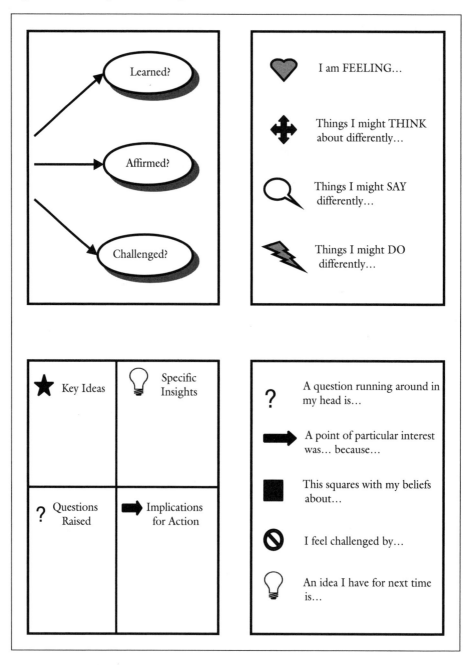

Finally, groups may choose to respond to a checklist or survey of specific group and individual behaviors as a way to reflect on their effectiveness. See Garmston and Wellman (1999) for a checklist that focuses on the seven norms of collaborative work shown in Figure 5.5. See also Thousand and Villa (2000) for a survey titled "Are We Really a Team?" and other tools used to prompt reflection and learning about the group process. An observer, who has noted group behavior and shares personal observations for the group's consideration, may lead the process.

Regardless of the specific method of reflection that is chosen, individuals and the group as a whole must reflect on their contributions if learning and improvement are to occur. Consider again that "adults do not learn from experience, they learn from processing experience" (Garmston & Wellman, 1997, p. 1). The varied strengths, experiences, and perspectives available in a group context have the potential to contribute substantially to group learning.

How Can Time Be Allocated for Learning Together?

Time is our most valuable, nonrenewable resource. We must use time wisely. Finding time for teachers to collaborate and learn together is a critical element for implementing and sustaining school improvement efforts (U.S. Department of Education, 1996). It has been identified as an essential structural condition within an organization to support both individual and collective learning (Donahoe, 1993; Louis, 1992; Raywid, 1993; Watts & Castle, 1993). Although having time to meet does not guarantee that collaboration will happen or that the time will be effectively used, not having time precludes the possibility of sustaining broader team and school collaboration efforts. Unless schools intentionally think about how they structure and use time, with special attention paid to scheduling collaborative time, teachers will tend to work alone or with one other colleague (Adelman, 1998).

Time is a resource that creates many contradictions in our lives. Although it is highly valued, many would question if we use our available time for the most valuable purposes. It is a finite resource that is blamed for an infinite number of frustrations. It is invisible, but our reactions to having a lack of time can be quite visible. Schein (1992) states that there is probably no more important factor in the analysis of an organization's culture than how it allocates and uses time. The pace of events, the rhythms of the building, the sequence in which things are done, and meeting agendas are all signs of what an organization or team values.

How staff members within schools choose to allocate their time runs the continuum from being totally focused on individual needs to being totally focused on collaborative needs. To establish permanent roots at either end of the spectrum, without acknowledging and scheduling time for the other, creates a system doomed for inadequacy. Total attention to individual time leads to teacher isolation, minimizing the value of sharing and learning with each other, and an inability to move new educational reforms within teams or organizations. Total attention to collaborative time means ignoring the value of individual reflection and, quite simply, the need to get routine chores completed. Teams and organizations need to move to a point at which individual and collective times are valued and included in their planning. Where we reach a balance, then we have the opportunity to positively expand team and organizational reflective practice.

"The perspective most needed . . . is that of time as a resource that can be shaped and reshaped to meet educational needs, rather than as the straitjacket into which teaching and learning have to be stuffed" (U.S. Department of Education, 1996, p. 11). How we organize time dictates, to a great extent, who can participate and what can be accomplished. Many schools across the country have identified finding time for teams to meet as a high priority and as a necessary step for supporting adult learning and organizational change. The North Central Regional Educational Laboratory (1994) identified five different strategies that schools were using to create time for teachers to meet and learn together. Schools are (a) freeing up temporary blocks of time, (b) purchasing additional professional time, (c) using common planning time more collaboratively, (d) restructuring individual school or district schedules, and (e) critically looking at how staff members are using the time they currently have available. Each of these strategies is explained in Table 5.3 along with specific examples of how they have been implemented in schools.

The key point to remember is that we will never just find time. Both individually and organizationally, the decision that time to learn is important must be followed up by figuring out how to make it happen. After clarifying specific reasons for meeting, then decisions need to be made about who needs to meet, how often meetings should be held, and when and where to meet. Given today's hectic pace, finding time for individual reflection can be difficult, but it also allows the most flexibility, because the only schedule to coordinate is our own. Finding time for reflecting with partners or groups is much more challenging. As a general rule, when figuring out time for small groups or teams, it is best to look for regular blocks of continuous time of no less than 45 minutes and, preferably, an hour or more. By scheduling meeting times on the school calendar in advance (e.g., scheduled by September for an entire school year), teachers and administrators are better able to resist the pressures to schedule other competing meetings. In the examples from the practice section that follows, we present a task-force process that was used to learn about and schedule time for team learning.

Reflection in Small Groups and Teams: Examples From Practice

Because of the many teams, committees, ad hoc interest groups, and governance groups in schools, embedding reflective practices within these structures could result in significant advances in educational practice. In this section, we describe

TABLE 5.3 Strategies and Examples of Time Allocated for Staff Learning

Strategy for Finding Time	*What Is It?*	*What Have Schools Done?*
Freed-Up Time	Temporary blocks of time were created for teachers through the use of substitutes, volunteers, or creative use of staff.	• They hired substitutes to release groups of teachers to meet every other week. • They scheduled special performances or assemblies so grade-level teams were free to meet during this time. • They arranged for a licensed staff member without regular classroom assignments to cover a classroom so that the classroom teacher has time to observe a peer teaching or to meet with a team member. • They created a reflection pool where individual teachers volunteer to cover colleagues' classes during their prep period, and teachers then have an opportunity for reflective practice. In exchange, teachers who have reflective practice place their names in the pool and cover colleagues' classes.
Purchased Time	Schools found creative ways to find and fund professional time, including use of early retirees, foundation funding, or contractual compensation—but these strategies tend to be temporary or transitional.	• The district negotiated teacher contracts that lengthen the teachers' day by 1 hour after students leave, creating time for teachers to meet. • Schools on year-round schedules dedicated 2 to 3 days during their intersession for teachers' meetings and staff development, with teachers receiving compensatory pay. • Districts offered compensatory pay for summer meeting and learning together. • Teachers stayed later one day a week to meet in reflective practice groups in exchange for being able to leave at the same time the students did on another day of the week.

(continued)

TABLE 5.3 Continued

Common Time	Schools developed team or grade-level schedules to create a common planning period or lunch period.	• They created brown-bag lunch groups that meet once a week to reflect on their practice. • In schools with 90-minute block schedule, 60 minutes of one planning period were dedicated to reflection on student learning, and 30 minutes went to daily business. • Schools targeted an available period of time, such as a common prep period, for infusing staff development into the school day.
Restructured or Rescheduled Time	School formally altered the school calendar or teaching schedule on a permanent basis.	• Special classes (e.g., art, music, gym) developed a series of half-day programs to periodically free up each grade-level team to meet. • Banking time—schools arranged for students to attend school several extra minutes on four days a week and to be released early on the fifth day, creating a block of time for teachers to meet during the school day. • They created a longer block of time by scheduling grade-level, common-planning periods or special events for immediately following or preceding a team's lunch period. • Teachers met in individual study groups after school throughout the school year in exchange for not having to attend the scheduled staff-development day. • They organized community service opportunities for all students on a half-day a week to create a block of time for teachers to meet. • Teachers arrived early at school once a week and students started later to create a block of time for teachers to meet.

specific examples of how reflective practices became a part of three different types of small groups that had schoolwide implications. We describe first the process employed by a task force charged with responsibility for figuring out time blocks for

TABLE 5.3 Continued

Better-Used Time	Staff examined current practices to see how schools are using the time they currently have to meet. When we meet, what do we meet about? Is our meeting time aligned with what we want to create? To accomplish? How can we best focus our time together on instruction and professional development?	• Weekly faculty meetings were reorganized so that normal school business is discussed once a month, and reflective practice groups or meetings are scheduled for the other 3 weeks and focus on student curriculum, instruction, and assessment. • Schools dedicated time when faculty is together to issues and discussions requiring group input; all other announcements and updates are shared through memos, e-mail, or voice mail.

SOURCE: Adapted from North Central Regional Educational Laboratory (1994).

instructional teams to meet in an elementary school. We describe next the way in which high school teachers voluntary formed a group to learn about integrating reading strategies into content-area instruction. Finally, we describe the process used to rethink space allocation in a high school. Across all three examples, several common elements emerge: an intentional design for promoting participation by group members; the use of reflection to promote learning and to monitor the group process and progress; and the role of the facilitator in initiating, continuously reflecting on, and guiding the process.

Time for Team-Learning Task Force

Plains Elementary School is a kindergarten-through-sixth-grade, urban school with about 650 students. The Plains staff was involved in developing collaborative teaching models to meet the needs of its diverse student population. Recognizing that a key factor for successful collaboration is a regular time for teaching teams to meet, reflect, and plan, a task force was formed to study ways of finding time to meet and to then make scheduling recommendations for the following school year. Reflection was an embedded part of the task-force process. Participants reflected on literature about time for team learning, they reflected on the current state of their schedule, they reflected forward about the impact of various scheduling options and strategies, and they reflected on the feedback from their peers.

The task-force participants were a representative group of 10 teachers from throughout the school, including teachers from primary and intermediate grades, special education, second languages, fine arts, the teachers union, and 2 teachers with previous experience developing Plains' schoolwide schedule. The principal was an ad hoc member of the task force and was kept abreast of the group's activities when unable to attend the meetings. The diverse membership of the task force increased the likelihood that schoolwide and cross-grade-level perspectives would be voiced and considered. It was hoped that this would result in recommendations that were both well conceived and well received.

Early in the task-force process, meetings were held off-site to keep participation focused (e.g., eliminate interruptions) and were held for half- or full days to allow sufficient time for reflection, dialogue, and learning together. The first few meetings were scheduled 3 to 4 weeks apart to allow time between sessions for participants to reflect on the options considered, the questions raised, and the directions proposed. Time between sessions also allowed task-force members to share information and obtain feedback from staff members not involved in the task-force meetings. Later on, when the process shifted from learning and idea generation to decision making and specific planning, meetings were held more closely together to sustain the momentum and to more expediently accomplish the scheduling task. A brief summary of the task-force sequence and process follows.

Meeting #1: Reflecting on Beliefs, Practices, and Research Participants reviewed research about why team meeting time was important and about how other schools have created blocks of time for teachers to meet and learn together. They also reflected on their individual beliefs about team time to reflect on practice and about current scheduling priorities and practices in their school. Through dialogue, participants considered how various time strategies might work in their school. No decisions were made. The process was intentionally kept open at this point.

Meeting #2: Identifying Principles for Decision Making As participants began to consider more specifically how time for team learning might be worked into the school schedule, confusion and tension emerged within the group. To schedule time for teams to reflect and learn together, they needed an understanding of what a team was. Would teams be organized by grade level? How would support personnel be assigned to teams? When would licensed personnel be scheduled to team teach in language arts blocks? As always, the greatest difficulties are in the details. The tension was an inevitable and necessary part of the process. Underlying assumptions and conflicts about working in isolation versus working in teams arose. There was also discomfort about what seemed to be an expanded role of the task force. They were not just scheduling, they were talking about the design of instructional teams throughout the school. Out of this meeting came two principles that guided future decisions made by the task force: (a) Program coherence and consistency must be increased for students and, as much as possible, for staff members;

and (b) instructional teams formed around grade levels must meet regularly to reflect and plan, focused on student learning—for example, short periods of time on a weekly basis to address immediate instructional issues and longer blocks of time every month or two to more comprehensively reflect and plan related to curriculum, instruction, and overall student performance.

Meeting #3: Updating the Principal   Task-force participants met briefly with the principal to provide an update on the process and progress. Two posters that summarized the previous meetings' dialogue were shared. It was apparent that despite the challenges in the previous meeting, substantial progress had been made. The principal agreed with the principles and encouraged the group to continue. The realization of progress and the support of the principal reenergized the teachers.

Meetings #4-6: Developing Specific Schedule Options   The fourth meeting was a full-day work session. Using paper cutouts of all of the staff members (color coded by position), task-force members began brainstorming about how the staff might be reorganized into grade-level teams composed of classroom teachers, specialists, and assistants. The staff cutouts were arranged and rearranged, with much conversation about advantages and disadvantages of different configurations. This activity helped to identify who needs to have the time to plan and meet. Task-force members then began working with specific scheduling ideas to support short weekly and long monthly blocks of time for team reflection and planning. Two short follow-up meetings (meetings 5 and 6) were held to fine-tune the two scheduling options that would be proposed to the entire staff.

Meetings With the Rest of the Staff: Soliciting Feedback   A meeting was scheduled with each grade level and with the fine arts teachers. The decision was made to meet in these small groups instead of with the staff as a whole in order to maximize the opportunity for participation and input. Selected task-force members and the facilitator led these meetings. The agenda was to inform about the task-force process and guiding principles, to propose the two schedule options, and to solicit feedback. No decisions were made in these small-group meetings. The feedback was compiled and then reviewed by the task force with final recommendations presented to the principal.

Making Final Recommendations   After receiving feedback, the task-force members made two recommendations to the whole staff. First, they recommended that all school-staff members reorganize around grade-level instructional teams that would meet once a week during their common prep period. This meant that specialists, such as teachers of special education and second languages, needed to realign so they spanned fewer grades and would be available to meet and plan with grade-level teachers. Second, they recommended that the school create a double-prep day once a month during which students in each grade would go to two consecutive preps. This would free grade-level teachers for an additional 100-minute block monthly to meet and plan. The staff and administration accepted both recommendations for implementation the following school year. Through a reflective process based on clearly defined guiding principles for decision making, the participants learned both individually and collectively and created a process and outcomes that the staff trusted and supported.

Reading Reflection Groups in High School

Teaching students to read has always been a priority in schools. In this era of increased school accountability, it is even more so. In one Midwestern, urban school district, teaching students to read is the top priority of the district. Their focus on reading intensified a few years ago when passing the state's basic standards test became a requirement for graduation. Following is a description of how one high school addressed this challenge, with reflection embedded in the program-development and staff-learning process.

Three years ago at Washington High School, many staff members believed that reading was a special education issue and not a schoolwide issue. Several special education teacher leaders made the bold statement that student success in reading was not owned by one department. They asserted that the school would not be successful reaching its student-reading goals if responsibility for this schoolwide issue was directed at one department. This group of teachers began working with school administrators to change staff perception about who had responsibility for teaching reading. A multiyear plan was developed to include all staff members and students in efforts to improve the quality of reading instruction across the school day in every class. The focus of the plan was to prepare all the teachers in the high school, across all disciplines, to provide quality reading instruction in their content areas. A group of special educators provided the leadership to move the issue of poor student-reading proficiency from "this is a problem for special education" to "this is a buildingwide issue."

During the first year, an intensive training program on reading instruction was offered during the summer by a local education cooperative. About a third of the Washington staff members attended the program. A key component then became follow-up. Voluntary, biweekly reading reflection groups were facilitated by one of the special educators. Between 15 and 20 teachers from a wide variety of disciplines (e.g., physics, math, health, special education) regularly attended these reflection sessions. Staff members who attended the summer staff-development session as well as those who were not able to attend were invited to participate in the follow-up reading reflection groups.

The reading reflection group met on Friday mornings before school. The focus of each session was determined by what the participants wanted to think and learn about. The special educators facilitated the conversation, intentionally modeling reflection and inquiry. Participants were encouraged to bring specific lessons to share so that everyone could learn from one another. Their sharing and application of ideas stimulated greater dialogue. Because the participants were from a wide variety of departments, the diversity in their backgrounds fueled broader application and learning for the group as a whole.

The facilitator purposefully incorporated a number of features into the reading reflection group. First, she made it fun. She believed the staff members would need to find the experience both enjoyable and valuable or they would not continue to return to the early-morning sessions. Second, she made sure that there was food at each meeting. Participants started their Friday eating and learning together. Third, she arranged for every session to begin with a short activity focused on reading. For example, a math teacher offered a short lesson on Latin roots and how he applied this knowledge in his math classes. After the presentation or activity, participants engaged in dialogue, sometimes related to the activity, sometimes related to some other aspect of embedding reading instruction in content-area curriculum.

Did the opportunities to reflect on reading make a difference? The teachers involved in the reading reflection group identified changes in two areas: professional relationships and instructional practice. Because of the participant diversity, new relationships were formed among teachers that extended across departments and grade levels. Participants also discovered in the group a safe place to learn with colleagues. They shared ideas and frustrations about integrating reading strategies into their content area instruction. Most important, they began to make changes in their own instructional practice. Through participation in the reading reflection groups, they developed greater knowledge about various reading strategies and how to use them in their classes. Evidence of progress in the area of reading resulted in the principal asking the teachers to develop and support a plan to increase student math proficiency.

New Ways of Thinking About Space Allocation

Allocating space at Newbury High School was a volatile topic. Historically, the administrators made all the decisions about space allocation. Staff members did not trust the decision making. Many staff members effectively maneuvered for better space. It was no coincidence that new teachers became the floaters who had to teach in several different rooms. In addition, space decisions were based on short-term projections instead of on long-term projections for each department. This resulted in a predictable cycle of putting up walls one year and tearing them down the next.

One teacher at Newbury was particularly bothered by how the decisions were made and was willing to facilitate an alternative decision-making process. She proposed that a volunteer committee study schoolwide issues and make specific recommendations about space allocation to the department chairpersons. The chairpersons would then make final decisions. It was this teacher's intent to design and facilitate a committee process that was inclusive and equitable so that recommendations would be viewed as fair. Committee members included an assistant principal and 13 staff members from a variety of departments who volunteered to be on the committee. Individuals who held key positions in the school (e.g., the head custodian, the athletic director, and the police liaison) were asked to participate. Described below are the major components of the process that emerged to address space allocation and also reflections on the process.

Developing Committee Group Norms and Expectations The space committee adopted the seven norms of collaborative work (Garmston & Wellman, 1997, 2000) (see Figure 5.5). These had been introduced previously in a schoolwide, staff-development session. Throughout the committee work, the norms were continually reviewed, especially during tense conversations. Also specifically reviewed were the differences between dialogue and discussion (see Chapter 2, pages 32-33) and how to engage in both forms of conversation. From the beginning, this set expectations that interactions would be respectful, that all members would be heard, and that reflection and learning with and from one another was essential. Committee members also made it a regular practice to keep colleagues updated about the process and progress of the committee work. A ritual called Rumor of the Week was instituted. At each committee meeting, members shared rumors that they had heard about the work of their space committee. This provided a forum for keeping in touch with staff perceptions while also creating opportunities to teach and model how to communicate effectively to dispel rumors. By being open and direct with others, participants found that trust in the people and in the process grew.

Clarifying Values for Decision Making Early in the committee process, soliciting input from all the teachers in the school generated values for decision making. All teachers received a survey asking them to identify the values on which space-utilization decisions should be made. Using the themes that emerged from the survey responses, department chairs then facilitated conversations with their department members about values for making decisions about space allocation. Values were rank ordered. The space-committee members compiled this feedback from each department and identified the top four values for decision making: (a) Use of space for instruction has priority over use of space for noninstructional purposes; (b) every teacher should teach in space that is conducive to student learning; (c) special consideration should be given to classes with unique curricular and instructional needs (e.g., art, science); and (d) teachers who teach five classes a day should have their classroom for the whole day. Overall, the intent was to align the available space with staff and programmatic needs in order to maximize the use of the facilities for student instruction.

Determining Short- and Long-Term Space Needs The second step in the process was to identify short- and long-term space needs. Again, all staff members were surveyed. Using an open-ended format, each person was asked to describe his or her needs for space and how the space would be used. These written reflections focused department-level conversations about the long- and short-term space needs of each department in the school. The purpose of this two-stage process was not only to prompt all staff members' reflections about their individual space needs but also, ultimately, to prompt reflection about space needs of the staff as a whole. This was an intentional effort by the committee to get people thinking outside their own realm of practice.

Becoming Familiar With All the Space After the values for decision making and the needs for space were identified, the committee took a walking tour of the whole school. The purpose was to increase the committee members' knowledge about the school's physical layout and facilities so they had a better understanding of the whole school for consideration in their decision-making process.

Engaging in Dialogue About Options As the committee began considering specific options for space utilization, the facilitator made sure that committee members had five pieces of information: (a) the values for decision making; (b) each department's short- and long-term needs; (c) the master schedule, including details about staffing assignments; (d) an accurate map of the building; and (e) a database of what room was used by whom during the school year.

With the information in hand, committee members engaged in dialogue about specific space use, room by room, floor by floor, and period by period. They made an effort to ensure understanding about why specific uses were suggested and also about inherent trade-offs with different options. Members saw a need to take a schoolwide perspective as they realized the domino effect throughout the building of making one simple change on space allocation. They created a color-coded map that visually displayed all staff or program changes. And the facilitator continually archived information and decisions to document the decision-making trail for future reference.

Making Decisions and Presenting Recommendations After extensive dialogue, the group began making decisions and constructed a plan that aligned with the agreed-on values and with the articulated, departmental, short- and long-term space needs. The plan and an accompanying rationale were presented to the administration and department chairs. The department chairs reviewed the recommendations and asked the committee to revisit a few issues that had raised staff members' concerns. Staff members involved with these issues dialogued with the space-allocation committee to better understand why these recommendations had been made. They ultimately gave their support to the plan, and the department chairs unanimously voted approval.

At the beginning of the second year, the facilitator solicited input from the committee members and from the department chairs about suggestions for changing the space-allocation, decision-making process. No changes were recommended. The committee's process of studying the issues, clearly articulating the values for making decisions, and being able to provide a rationale for its recommendations are now accepted and valued practices within the school. Although specific individuals may not agree with every recommendation, the teachers trust the process, so they trust and honor the recommendations.

Reflecting on the Space Allocation Outcomes and Process   Throughout the space committee process, there was ongoing reflection and dialogue. The committee's reflective process was an ongoing learning experience for all members. They learned how to think outside of the box and take a schoolwide view as they examined issues that directly affected the work of all staff members. In doing so, they understood more about what other staff members do and how their work contributes to the high school as a whole. Individuals throughout the school established new relationships. This assisted in the movement away from a turf culture to a broader and more inclusive approach to making decisions that affect the entire organization. Committee members learned how to organize and participate in a process that is fair and ethical. With the committee and within departments, dialogue became a valued means of interaction. This is particularly noteworthy given that volunteer, issue-based groups can attract people whose primary interest is protection of their own turf, advocacy for their own views. By making public the norms of interaction and the values by which decisions were made, the group achieved appropriate pressure for adherence to expectations.

Reflection in Small Groups and Teams: More Ideas to Consider

Some of the examples and ideas for reflecting on your own (Chapter 3) and with partners (Chapter 4) can be effective when applied to groups as well. Mapping (Chapter 3) and action research (Chapter 4) are two such examples. Described below is a menu of ideas for promoting reflection to improve practice in the context of groups. Many of the ideas and strategies overlap. The learning process most strongly featured throughout the examples is reflection through dialogue with colleagues. Some of the examples are drawn from the literature, and readers are encouraged to seek the original references for more specific information.

Metaphors

Metaphors (also described for individual application in Chapter 3) offer a way to give meaning to an experience or object symbolically. "Metaphor is a transfer of meaning from one object to another on the basis of perceived similarity" (Taggart & Wilson, 1998, p. 188). Hagstrom et al. (2000) used metaphor to write about

their experiences as teachers. They completed the sentence stem, "Teaching is like
. . ." with responses that included the ocean, making bread, and geology. They
then wrote short essays to explain further their choice of metaphor. Shared use of
metaphors enriched their individual and collective understandings of life as a
teacher. This process "resulted in some of the most joyful and most thought pro-
voking writing we have ever done" (Hagstrom et al., 2000, p. 25).

Metaphors can be an effective and fun way to close a group session by eliciting
higher-level thinking and application. One way to do this is to invite each small
group to write down four nouns—for example, cat, chocolate, bicycle, bus. Then
ask that they select one of the nouns to complete the following sentence: X is like X
because X. Here are two examples: (a) Dialogue is like chocolate because it is rich,
you share it with people who are close to you, and you want it to last a long time;
(b) coteaching is like riding a bicycle because it takes two strong wheels working
together to get anywhere.

A final idea for use of metaphor in groups is to capture both current and desired future states. For example, during initiation into reflective practice, a team of
teachers was asked to identify a metaphor for how reflection felt very early in the
learning process and how they hoped it would feel by the end of the year. Here is a
sample response: "Reflective practice now feels like an elephant because it is big,
heavy, bulky, and slow. In the spring, I hope it will feel like a monkey—flexible,
flowing, responsive, and moving between different levels."

Talking Cards

Talking Cards is a strategy for obtaining full but anonymous participation in a
group context. Each member is provided with index cards and a felt-tip pen or
marker, the same color for everyone. A question is posed to the group, and members write their responses on index cards (one idea or response per card). All the index cards are then collected and laid out for all group members to see, usually on
the floor or a large table. Together, group members sort cards into clusters or
themes to make sense of all the ideas shared. Once all the cards are sorted, the
group labels the clusters. This results in a comprehensive and organized presentation of the group's collective perspectives. With a full disclosure of this sort, the
group can then make well-informed decisions.

We use this strategy regularly with groups of teachers in schools. It has been
particularly helpful in structuring reflection on and for action in the middle and at
the end of the school year. For example, we used a variation of this process to help
teacher teams of general educators, special educators, and second-language teachers to reflect on their first few months of team teaching. First, they were asked to
outline on poster paper what their team teaching looked like. This part of the process focused on describing the current state, or the what-is part, of the reflection
process. Specifically, they responded to the question, "If you were to explain your
approach to team teaching to another school, what features would you point out?"

In teacher teams, they bulleted the features of their approach on poster paper. The various approaches were posted on the wall and explained to other teams.

Second, the talking cards strategy was used. Each teacher was asked to respond to four questions, individually and anonymously, using different-colored index cards to respond to each question. This part of the reflection process prompted perspective sharing about how well the team teaching was working or not. The questions were:

- What have been the advantages of team teaching for students? (Responses written on green cards)

- What have been the disadvantages of team teaching for students? (Responses written on red cards)

- What have been the advantages of team teaching for the adult team members? (Responses written on yellow cards)

- What have been the disadvantages of team teaching for the adult team members? (Responses written on blue cards)

The teachers could contribute as many responses as they wanted for each question by writing each thought or response on an individual card. When all the teachers within a team finished writing, the cards were collected, sorted by color, displayed on the table or floor, and then sorted into clusters as a group activity. The clusters were then labeled. Labels were written on white index cards and placed with their respective clusters. For example, some of the cluster labels that were related to advantages for students included "modeling from peers," "closer relationships with classmates," and "all teachers know all students better." Cluster labels for adult team-member advantages included "learning ideas from other teachers," "feel more connected to team members," and "better communication and support."

Third, each group began to inquire about what this means, the so-what and now-what aspects of the reflection process. Questions were asked, such as, "What is our overall assessment of how things have been going? What strengths do we want to maximize? How might we reduce the disadvantages? What might be our next steps for improving how we teach and learn together?" These piles of cards can also be typed to provide a written record for more reflection at a later point or reflection back at the end of the school year. The conversation that occurs in the sorting, clustering, and inquiry aspects of this process is invaluable. This is when the individual and collective group learning occurs.

Six Hats

Another reflection strategy that assists groups in thinking about how to move forward is referred to as Six Hats. Proposed by de Bono (1970), this process requires groups to consider the implications of potential actions or interventions from six different perspectives. For example, as a planning team, a group of teachers posed the following question to themselves: "If we were to propose this reflective practice in our high school, what should we be thinking about in terms of implementation supports and potential issues?" The principal led the conversation by actually wearing six different-colored hats and guiding the group's thinking about each perspective:

- The white hat symbolizes data: What does research say about reflective practice? How effective has it been and in what specific circumstances? How much does it cost to implement?

- The yellow hat symbolizes sunshine: There will be a better appreciation of differences. This will boost staff morale! Students will benefit from improved instruction. Problem-solving and perspective-taking skills will increase.

- The black hat symbolizes caution: This will be a hard idea to sell. The staff will see it as another fad. The site council will want to see the budgetary implications. People who think they are doing well may be disillusioned; they may even leave. It is going to take a lot of time and resources to get it off the ground.

- The red hat symbolizes emotion: Some of the teachers are going to panic; others will see it as touchy-feely nonsense. People will feel so much more connected to one another. I am excited about all the possibilities.

- The green hat symbolizes growth: We will all learn so much. I will become a better teacher, maybe even a better person. This will be a challenge, but I could use some new ways of thinking about meaningful assessment. Reflecting on our teaching with other staff members will result in a wider array of instructional strategies.

- The blue hat symbolizes process: We will have to put together information to share with the staff and site council. What team of teachers could examine the schedule to figure out when groups could meet? A kickoff during workshop week could get us off to a good start next school year. There will need to be a lead team to keep this on the front burner.

By engaging in conversation from each of these different perspectives, the group was able to anticipate needs and potential responses. This process supported their reflection-for-action and resulted in a plan about how to move forward. In their debriefing about the six-hats process, participants shared insights about the type of perspective they typically bring to a conversation. Some recognized that they quickly assume a cautious or data-based way of thinking. Others respond positively, because they hone in on the growth potential. Still others move right away to planning a process for getting things done. These personal insights were very constructive. Each member could see strengths in the varied perspectives and recognize the variation as reflecting individual diversity.

Think Tank

A group of five elementary teachers and three university professors developed a discourse community that they referred to as a think tank, which focused on learning more about how children acquire new vocabulary (Henry et al., 1999). They met for dinner every 6 to 8 weeks throughout a school year to reflect on their experiencing and thinking about promoting vocabulary with students. "Through dialogue, the members of this group shared their expertise over time, building a common voice and a common knowledge base" (p. 258). Five expectations emerged as important in their group learning: safety built on trust, dialogue as a means of learning, collaboration among equals, personal commitment, and time together. They identified several functions of their interactions: description, analysis, expansion, summarizing, and defining. Outcomes indicated enhanced knowledge related to the content focus (vocabulary learning in students) and the reflection and learning process.

Interactive Reflective Teaching

Seminars that included preservice teachers, cooperating teachers and principals, and college faculty members provided a means for interactive reflection on teaching practice (Diss, Buckley, & Pfau, 1992). "Reflective teaching is an introspective process of examining one's own teaching behavior" (p. 28). The focus of reflection was the instructional decision-making process of the teachers to gain insight about decision making in action. "Reflective teachers identified the strengths and weaknesses of their instructional decisions through inquiry, observations, peer interaction, and analysis to improve classroom decision making" (p. 28). The interactive seminars occurred four times in a semester. In addition to attending the seminars, preservice teachers observed experienced teachers for a total of 16 hours over the course of a semester. Prior to the observations, they identified specific questions about teaching that guided their observations. In the words of the authors,

> Participants' reactions to the program were extremely favorable. Teachers reported that the seminars contributed to their professional growth by: (a) increasing their awareness of the need to think critically and creatively about decision making; (b) broadening their teaching repertoires; (c) providing confirmation of their effective teaching methods; and (d) reinforcing the value of ongoing reflective teaching. (Diss et. al., 1992, p. 30)

Teachers rarely take the time to converse with one another about their practice, making the interactive design of the program especially valuable. Also of value was the participant mix of preservice and experienced teachers.

Self-Organized Teacher-Support Groups

In the reflective practice literature is a lot of support for self-organized learning groups. Rich (1992) reports on voluntary teachers' groups that were self-organized to meet teacher needs for support around curriculum and instruction. This particular effort grew out of teacher frustration with the manner in which a district-sponsored, all-day workshop was conducted. One of the teachers stated,

> We needed time to talk about how the program might look in practice. The curriculum was readable and we knew the theory, but we wanted to talk to other teachers about what to do with the new materials and about how to manage the program. We were also concerned about balancing the program to address skills and children's needs. (p. 33)

Two teachers asked others who shared this frustration to join with them in planning their own professional-development program. Two weeks later, seven teachers went to the first meeting at one teacher's home. Participants decided to meet monthly and to include in their monthly meeting both discussion of a professional reading and sharing of classroom practices and learning. Responsibility for choosing and distributing articles was rotated. Members were also encouraged to bring a friend.

Over the years, the group developed a newsletter that compiled their learning about effective classroom practice, shared their learning at faculty meetings, and presented workshops to other interested teachers. As the group grew in size, subgroups were formed to keep the size manageable, but participants continued to meet as a whole group every couple of months. Eventually, there were voluntary teacher-support groups in every section of the city.

Teacher Dialogues

Arnold (1995) describes teacher dialogues that were used to reflect on instructional practice. This approach is grounded in a constructivist view of knowledge generation. The dialogues were held at least twice each month during the school day and included four to five teachers and a leader. Initially, the leader assumed primary responsibility for facilitating conversation by posing reflective questions. Topics for reflection varied depending on teacher interests and needs. For example, the dialogues were used as a forum for examining and discussing application of state-curricular frameworks. Research was frequently reviewed in the dialogues as well. On some occasions, teachers had the opportunity to observe one another teaching. This enriched the subsequent dialogues. The dialogues were considered a successful approach to learning when teachers

> (a) feel comfortable enough to reveal problems in their own instructional program and seek solutions from the groups; (b) bring in ideas they found to be especially successful with their class and urge others to try them; (c) volunteer to share new research; (d) invite the group to see a lesson in their class; and (e) . . . [find a] need for the leader decreases because of the group's increased capacity for leadership. (p. 35)

The author identified four factors to consider in the development of teacher dialogues: schedule time during the school day; use reflective questioning as a way to focus on instructional practice and student learning; select a knowledgeable and skillful facilitative leader who is a good teacher; and evaluate the effectiveness of the dialogues, including an oral reflection at the end of each session.

Video Clubs

Videotapes provide an "objective record of what actually took place" in a specific instructional context (Wallace, 1991, p. 8, as cited in Bailey, Curtis, & Nunan, 1998, p. 553). Sherin (2000) explains that video clubs "are opportunities for teachers to review their classroom interactions in ways that are different from their standard daily practices" (p. 36). Groups of four teachers gather monthly to watch and then converse about short segments (about 10 minutes) of videotaped teaching. The purpose is to examine and reflect on, not evaluate, instructional practice more specifically. Use of video allows teachers to narrow their view of classroom interactions. Unlike being in the act of teaching, the teacher does not have to attend the entire group. Individual or small groups of students can be observed more carefully. Teachers can also observe how they responded, then consider both why they responded in that way and alternatives. A significant finding was that the "teachers reported not only increased understanding when reflecting on video, but also paying more attention to student responses during instruction" (Sherin, 2000, p. 37). In a study of inservice and preservice teachers, 87% (of 87 teachers) stated that "seeing themselves on videotape had made them aware of habits and mannerisms that they were now trying to change" (Wallace, 1979, p. 13). This indicates that reflection-on-action subsequently increased reflection-in-action.

Teacher Book Clubs

Goldberg and Pesko (2000) initiated teacher book clubs, based on a belief that literacy instruction would improve if teachers themselves were involved in reading and reflecting on literature. The selections were pleasure reading, not professional reading. This recreated an opportunity to personalize the experience of literature and better understand the range of reading styles and reading responses of students. "We read and discuss literature, analyze our personal preferences for reading, reflect on classroom practices, and modify classroom practices on the basis of what we have learned" (p. 39).

Reflection Roundtables

We began the use of reflection roundtables as a way of gathering medium-sized groups of teachers within our partnership schools to engage in conversations about a variety of issues and topics. Early in our work with one school, we needed a schoolwide perspective about how general and special educators worked together, the strengths and challenges in their present way of providing services to students with disabilities, and the areas or ideas for improvement that would make a difference for students. We did not want to hear from only a handful of teachers or lead team, and we did not want to interact with the entire faculty at once (e.g., in a faculty meeting). We wanted the interaction to be a reflection and learning opportunity for all those involved. We held a series of three roundtable conversations, each had a mix of 8 to 12 teachers and lasted about 90 minutes. These roundtables increased our understanding and the understanding of all the teachers engaged in the conversation. It also was the start of trust and relationship building. The reflection roundtable continued to be used as a way to solicit input, feedback, and, ultimately, decision making about new directions for service provision.

Another use of reflection roundtables occurred in a school that had successfully piloted a general-educator and special-educator coteaching model of instruction during language arts and math. In the spring of the pilot year, the entire faculty needed to be involved in a conversation about implementation and outcomes of the coteaching model. A series of roundtable conversions were held with small groups of teachers, this time homogeneously grouped. We sat around small tables and asked participants what they wanted to know about the pilot. We shared what the coteaching looked like in each of the pilot classrooms, what the teachers thought about it, and the effects experienced by students. We were careful to disclose a balanced view of the process and outcomes. Participants asked questions and expressed concerns and special considerations. The cumulative learning and perspectives offered during the roundtable conversations were then (anonymously) shared during an extended faculty meeting. The faculty talked further in small groups during the meeting and, ultimately, made the decision to expand coteaching in specific ways and with specific cautions.

Reflection roundtables have been an effective means of sharing, learning, understanding, and relationship building that, ultimately, support decision making. They offer opportunities for dialogue before moving toward decision making. They have been effective because of the relatively small group size, intentional group composition (heterogeneous or homogeneous depending on purpose), high degrees of participation, an initial focus on reflection and inquiry through dialogue, and multiple gatherings and conversations before decision making.

Getting Started With Reflection in Small Groups and Teams

We opened this chapter suggesting that many educators are on meeting overload. Recently, we asked a group of graduate students to create a matrix of the groups (e.g., teams) that meet in their respective schools. When they returned with their matrices, we were all astounded by the huge amount of time spent in meetings. There is no shortage of meetings. One aspect of the analysis was to identify the groups that were effective and why. The findings were both disappointing and enlightening. Disappointing because few groups were meeting about instruction and because very little learning was occurring for the group members. Enlightening because it was crystal clear that a shift was needed in priorities about how face-to-face time was spent with colleagues. We would like to suggest that the first priority for teachers spending time together should be reflection and learning focused on students and instruction.

To guide your thinking about and moving forward with reflection in groups and teams, we invite you to contemplate the following questions.

- What is the purpose of the group? What is the focus for learning? What are the desired outcomes? Which students are likely to benefit from the learning that occurs within this group of educators? How conflicted is the focus of the group?

- How structured will the group process need to be to address the given purpose? Is there a specific time frame that must be honored? What kind of design will best promote participation, learning, and accomplishment?

- Should an existing group or team of individuals convene? Should additional individuals be included? Does a new group need to be configured?

- Who should be part of the group? Who has an important perspective to share? Who will be expected to follow through with the outcomes?

- How big should the group be? If a large number of people are involved, how can their participation be promoted? When might we need to consider breaking into smaller groups?

- Do we need to assign specific group roles? Should they be rotated? Who will assume lead roles in the group? Might two teachers share responsibility for organizing, communicating, and preparing? Is a facilitator needed? If so, who might that be?

- Do the group members know one another well? If they do not, how should we explicitly focus on developing relationships and trust?

- What experiences do group members have with reflection and learning? How intentional do we need to be about development of individual and group capacities for reflecting, learning, and working together?

- How will we determine the effectiveness of the group process? What content and process reflection strategies might we use?

The Chapter Reflection: Capturing Your Thoughts form (Figure 5.7) on the next page can be used to jot down your thoughts in response to these questions. You may also want to write down the most important learning that occurred for you as you read this chapter.

When reflecting in groups or teams, the potential emerges to influence more broadly the educational practices within and throughout the school. This potential significantly increases when multiple groups and teams embed reflective practices in their work and when efforts expand to include the vast majority of individuals and groups in a school. The sustainability of groups depends on four factors: a meaningful and continuing purpose; positive and productive working relationships; the opportunity for learning, growth, and contribution; and the outcomes realized by students. These factors provide a framework for evaluating the effectiveness, or likelihood of effectiveness, in schools.

Figure 5.7. Chapter Reflection: Capturing Your Thoughts

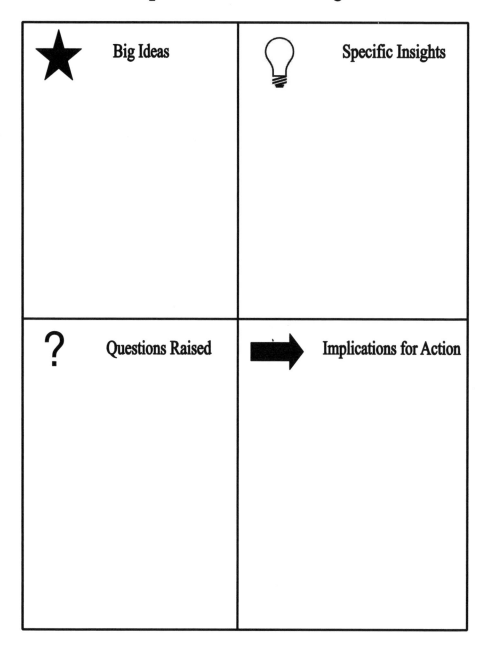

Capture Your Thoughts

6

Schoolwide Reflection

Reflective organizations are places where people can
bring themselves fully to work. Being fully present at
work is a remarkable and powerful experience, all the
more so if one contrasts it experientially with its
opposite, disconnection or alienation.

—Ellen Schall (1995, p. 207)
Learning to Love the Swamp

A principal who was new to a building arrived at a faculty meeting several
weeks into the school year and announced, "Please get your coats and meet
me in the parking lot." Somewhat perplexed, the faculty complied with this re-
quest. As soon as everyone reconvened in the parking lot, the principal explained
that in his short time in the building, he had noticed that the real meetings among
faculty occurred in the parking lot. He wanted to have a real meeting, one in which
faculty members actively participated in a process of sharing, listening, inquiring,
and learning. How do we get more real meetings occurring in schools? How do we
shift the focus of face-to-face time, at faculty meetings and elsewhere, to opportunities for learning? What topics of interaction would inspire ongoing reflection and
inquiry on a schoolwide basis? What conditions would promote honest, open ex-
changes among staff members? Who leads the process? Where do you start?

Costa and Kallick (2000) suggest that "every school's goal should be to habit-
uate reflection throughout the organization—individually and collectively, with
teachers, students, and the school community" (p. 60). Indeed, the greatest potential for reflective practice to improve schools lies with the collective thinking, inquiry, understanding, and action that can result from schoolwide engagement, the
outer level of the reflective practice spiral (Figure 6.1). Facilitating reflective practices at this level, however, is much more complex than at the individual, partner,
or small-group level.

121

Figure 6.1. The Reflective Practice Spiral With Schoolwide Level of Reflection Highlighted

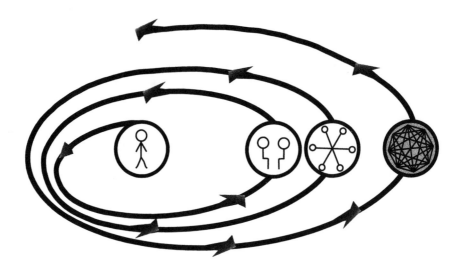

Kim (1993) offers insights about the relationship between individual and organizational learning, emphasizing the increasing complexity at the organizational level:

> Organizational learning is more complex and dynamic than a mere magnification of individual learning. The level of complexity increases tremendously when we go from a single individual to a large collection of diverse individuals. Issues of motivation and reward, for instance, which are an integral part of human learning, become doubly complicated within organizations. Although the meaning of the term *learning* remains essentially the same as in the individual case, the learning process is fundamentally different at the organizational level. (p. 40)

What would schoolwide reflective practice look like? What would you see and hear that would suggest the presence of genuine inquiry about practice? Schoolwide reflection does not mean that everyone is reflecting on the same thing in the same way at the same time. At times, most staff members may participate in a major schoolwide focus. More often, reflection will be used in a variety of ways to promote staff learning. Envision lots of groups learning throughout a school, some of which are ongoing whereas others form around a specific task and then disband when the task is completed.

Here are some examples of what schoolwide reflective practice might look like. An entire school staff may be involved in study groups on a common topic, such as reading in the content areas or performance assessment. Interdisciplinary groups might form to share disciplinary expertise and to create a set of integrated student outcomes that would be addressed within each of the content areas. Cross-grade-level teams might explore the best practices for effective student transitions between grades or schools. Some issues require schoolwide attention and participation, so group composition should be intentionally designed to connect people across grade levels or curricular areas and to bring forth different perspectives. Such efforts result in relationships forming among individuals who may not typically cross paths during a school day. It is not possible or necessary to include every staff member in every learning opportunity. What matters most is that all staff members are involved in some type of learning or shared-work initiative in addition to being committed to their own learning and professional development. Why is this so important? Reflection is important because it causes a person to think more deeply about an issue, to take into account more possibilities, and to consider the consequences of different courses of action when planning. As reflection increases, errors decrease (Argyris, 1977). More thought, better decisions.

The ultimate goal of schoolwide reflective practice is continuous improvement of practice in order to increase student learning. This requires alignment and continuity for students across grade levels and curricular areas. In many schools, students are their own sources of continuity in their school experiences. Alignment and continuity are achieved as the web of relationships (Figure 1.4, page 18) strengthens and broadens the school community. As the web becomes stronger, all students are more likely to receive a coherent, high-quality education. Fewer will fall through the open spaces in the web. Increasing the strength of community requires intentional focus by the formal and informal leaders in a school.

In this chapter, we describe special considerations for reflective practice at the schoolwide level. As suggested earlier, success at this level in the reflective practice spiral is more complicated than at previous levels and requires more intentional focus on design. We describe the journey of two schools that used reflection as a foundation for various school-improvement efforts. Finally, we present a menu of additional ideas for schoolwide reflective practice and offer a set of questions to prompt thinking about how to get started at this complicated and potentially powerful level of organizational change.

Special Considerations for Schoolwide Reflection

There is no one right way to do reflective practice on a schoolwide basis. In fact, the inherent messiness of schoolwide design and facilitation of learning could easily overwhelm one with possibilities and options. The ready-fire-aim approach advocated by Fullan and Stiegelbauer (1991) suggests that a certain amount of planning and preparation is appropriate but that the most important and informed decisions emerge from ongoing reflection throughout the implementation process. Just as navigating a plane or sailboat involves a process of continual readjustment to stay on course, so too does facilitating ongoing reflection and learning among staff members in a school. There are, however, considerations that serve as a foundation for moving forward with schoolwide reflective practice. We describe three major areas of consideration to guide the thinking, planning, and ongoing adjustments: (a) creating professional learning communities, (b) facilitating school change for improvement, and (c) fostering shared leadership. In addition, the considerations for promoting reflection in groups or teams presented in Chapter 5 apply to schoolwide reflective practices as well, because "schoolwide" frequently means many groups whose members are drawn from throughout the school.

Creating Professional Learning Communities

Over the past decade, emphasis has increased on schoolwide, as opposed to isolated, improvement efforts. Isolated efforts (i.e., initiatives taken on by individual teachers, grade levels, or content areas) typically result in only isolated improvements, with few cumulative gains realized once students move on from those experiences. Spread of effects to other groups of students is unlikely without intentional efforts to design and implement new practices with those students. This is one of the major reasons for the emergence of practices intended to recreate schools as professional learning communities in which all members actively participate in continuous learning and improvement efforts.

> Many of us have found that the existence of collaborative work cultures (or professional learning communities) makes a difference in how well students do in schools . . . we now have a much better idea of what is going on inside the black box of collaborative schools. (Fullan, 2000b, p. 581)

In successful schools, researchers have found that the existence of a professional learning community and an intentional, ongoing focus on student work result in continuous improvements in instructional practice (Newmann & Wehlage, 1995). Professional learning communities appear to be both a facilitator and benefactor of reflection.

Hord (1997) summarized the findings from numerous studies to identify outcomes that resulted for students and staff when schools organized themselves as professional learning communities. Students had lower rates of absenteeism, a reduced drop-out rate, and fewer cuts of classes. Also evident were larger academic gains in math, science, history, and reading. Increases in learning were also shown to be more equitably distributed throughout the school (in smaller high schools), and the achievement gaps between students with different backgrounds were smaller. For staff, the findings clustered around improvements in instructional practice and around overall professional conditions of teaching. Improvements in instructional practice included increased commitments to the mission and goals of the school; a heightened understanding of teachers' roles in helping all students achieve expectations; shared responsibility for student development and success; new knowledge and beliefs about practice, given the opportunity to learn together; and advances in making adaptations for students. Improvement in the professional conditions of teaching included reduced isolation among teachers, a higher likelihood of being well informed and professionally renewed, a greater commitment to making significant and lasting changes, and a greater likelihood of undertaking major systemic change. Also reported were higher levels of satisfaction and morale and, like the students, lower rates of absenteeism.

As educators join together to learn and improve practice, their sense of efficacy and support seems to increase. This is a critical capacity in the development of schoolwide initiatives. Teachers must believe that positive and significant change is possible. As they join together, they begin to realize that others, like themselves, are interested in and committed to significant and positive improvements in the teaching and learning process. Together, improvement seems possible. Alone, improvement seems less probable.

Based on a comprehensive review of research and related literature, Kruse, Louis, and Bryk (1995) propose a framework for analyzing school-based professional community (Figure 6.2). This framework identifies purported benefits, defining characteristics, and organizational supports of professional learning communities in schools. The framework can be used to design, troubleshoot, and reflect on progress being made toward creating professional learning communities. The authors suggest three, interrelated, potential benefits that result from the establishment of professional learning communities: increased teacher efficacy and empowerment, increased satisfaction that emerges from the dignity of being treated as respected and valued professionals, and collective responsibility for student learning. Also identified are five characteristics that define the presence of a school-based professional community: shared norms and values, reflective dialogue, deprivatization of practice (i.e., more open sharing about practices), a focus on student learning, and collaboration. Most important among these characteristics is the focus on student learning.

> Public conversations concerning practice within schools needs to focus on four topics: academic content, the intelligent use of generic teaching strategies, the development of students, and the social conditions of schooling and issues of equity and justice. (Kruse et al., 1995, p. 30)

The structure and social resources identified in the framework are required to support the development of school-based professional communities. Among these supports are specific and important considerations for the design of schoolwide reflective practices, such as times to meet and talk, communication structures, and

Figure 6.2. Emerging Framework for School-Based Professional Community

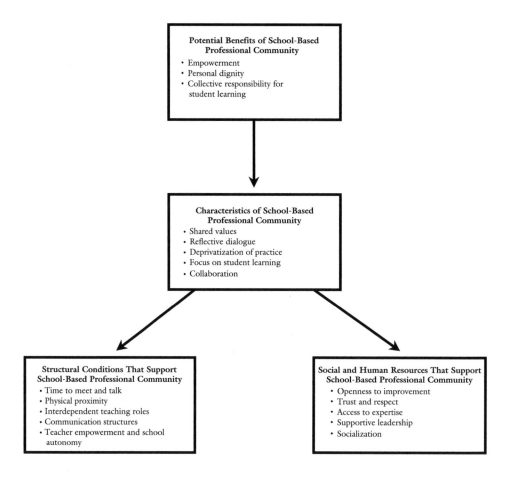

SOURCE: Kruse, S. D., Louis, K. S., & Bryk, A. (1995). "An Emerging Framework for Analyzing School-Based Professional Community." In K. S. Louis & S. D. Kruse (Eds.), *Professionalism and Community: Perspectives on Reforming Urban Schools* (p. 25). Copyright © by Corwin Press. Reprinted by permission of Corwin Press, Inc.

supportive leadership. These supports will be evident in the examples from practice described later in this chapter.

The school-based, professional-community framework (Kruse et al., 1995) has guided our thinking about the design and evaluation of various school improvement initiatives, including those that involve reflective practices. One modification that has proved useful is to reverse the direction of the arrows so that they point up, instead of down. This inversion emphasizes the foundational nature of the support level in the framework. Without the structural, social, and human-resource supports, the characteristics and benefits of professional learning communities will not emerge.

Facilitating Change at the Organizational Level

Promoting schoolwide reflection and learning requires an organizational perspective on facilitating change for improvement. This includes both an understanding of how individual staff members respond to change and an understanding of how to design and support change efforts from an organizational perspective. Moore and Gergen (1989) describe four stages of staff response to change: shock, defensive retreat, acknowledgement, and, finally, adaptation. Shock emerges when change is seen as a threat. Facilitators of the change process need to provide the opportunity for concerns to be expressed. They should also identify role expectations—and what is and is not going to change for them. The defensive retreat takes form as an investment of energy in maintaining the usual way of doing things. Again, facilitators need to clarify expectations, roles, and what will and will not change. As participants begin to see value in what is coming, they acknowledge the change and begin to let go of their retreat stance. Sadness is gradually replaced by excitement, and energy is redirected to accomplishing new tasks. In this phase, facilitators encourage taking risks and emphasize that adopting the change is a learning process. Adaptation is indicated as most staff members appear to be positioned to assume the new roles and are beginning to establish new routines.

Hord, Rutherford, Huling-Austin, and Hall (1987) presented the Concerns-Based Adoption Model (CBAM), which is still considered a valid template for understanding and supporting individual educators through a change process (Horsley & Loucks-Horsley, 1998). The model indicates that individuals are concerned first about how the change will affect them personally: "How will my practices have to change? What will be expected of me?" Next, concerns emerge about managing all the tasks involved in successfully implementing a new program: "How will I get everything prepared? How can I manage all the pieces? Which tasks should come first?" Finally, concerns shift to considering the impact of the change: "What is happening for students as a result of this change? How can I improve implementation? I wonder how others are working with this new program and what they are learning?" The CBAM recognizes that the individual is central to the change process and that supports for teachers should align with their concerns. Task concerns, for example, should be supported with specific information and examples about how to manage and implement the new practice. Information about why the practice is recommended would not feel supportive when the teacher is trying to figure out how to do it. Impact concerns might be supported by providing opportunities for teachers who have begun experimenting with implementation to talk together about what they are learning and how to refine, extend, and share their practices.

Shifting now to organizational-level change considerations, we have found that numerous models support the design and implementation of improvement initiatives such as reflective practice. One model that we have found to be useful is the Managing Complex Change model (Figure 6.3) presented by Ambrose (1987)

Figure 6.3. Adaptation of Ambrose's (1987) *Managing Complex Change* Model

Vision	+	Skills	+	Incentives	+	Resources	+	Action Plan	→	CHANGE
		Skills	+	Incentives	+	Resources	+	Action Plan	→	CONFUSION
Vision	+			Incentives	+	Resources	+	Action Plan	→	ANXIETY
Vision	+	Skills	+			Resources	+	Action Plan	→	FRUSTRA-TION
Vision	+	Skills	+	Incentives	+			Action Plan	→	GRADUAL CHANGE
Vision	+	Skills	+	Incentives	+	Resources			→	FALSE STARTS

SOURCE: Villa, R. A., & Thousand, J. S. (Eds.) (2000). *Restructuring for Caring and Effective Education: Piecing the Puzzle Together* (2nd ed., p. 97). Baltimore: Paul H. Brookes.

and adapted by Villa and Thousand (1992), and by Knoster, Villa, and Thousand (2000). This deceptively simple framework clearly identifies key elements of a successful change process and, perhaps more important, the outcomes that can be expected when each element is not addressed. The elements are vision, skills, incentives, resources, and action plan. Without vision, an initiative is not meaningfully grounded in a desirable future state or purpose, which results in confusion. What is this supposed to look like? Why are we doing this anyway? Without skills, anxiety grows as staff members are asked to perform in new ways without the opportunity to learn new behavior and understanding. Without incentives, such as engagement being recognized and the educational value being specified, change is adopted gradually, if at all. Without resources, such as time for learning and money for materials or training (if appropriate), the system has insufficient capacity to support change, and frustration results. Without a plan that is thoughtfully crafted and continually modified in response to feedback about progress, false starts occur. False starts eventually zap the energy of even the most well-intentioned and enthusiastic educators. The team of individuals who assume responsibility for planning and oversight of schoolwide reflection and learning opportunities can use the Managing Complex Change model as a framework for ongoing reflection and problem solving as the professional learning community develops.

Fostering Shared Leadership

Shared leadership that involves the active support of formal and informal school leaders is known to be a key facilitating factor in school improvement initiatives (Bryk, Camburn, & Louis, 1999; Lambert, 1998; Marks & Louis, 1999). One responsibility of leaders is to foster leadership throughout the organization. One person or a few administrators cannot possibly be the only ones concerned with leadership. Leadership must be fostered within the faculty, noncertified staff members, students, parents, and community. Leadership is a process that needs continual attention. As long as improvement is dependent on a single person or a few people or outside directions and forces, it will fail (Lambert, 1998). The leadership in a building, whether vested in an individual or group, exerts primary control over resources that affect implementation of reflective practices, such as schedule, assignments of classes and committees, use of space, and decision making about staff-development resources. The ways in which these resources are allocated affects the ways in which the school operates, including how reflection and learning among staff members are supported. By tapping both formal and informal leaders, the much-needed resource of a broad perspective on the school is brought forward and greatly enhances the design and implementation process. Please note that in the brief review of literature that follows, the leadership role of principals is featured more prominently than the leadership role of teachers. This uneven presentation reflects the disproportionately few number of studies available on teachers as leaders, despite the growing recognition of their essential role in successful school improvement (Fullan, 1993; Lieberman & Miller, 1999; Moller & Katzenmeyer, 1996).

Crow (1998) reviewed studies that focused on leadership and leadership roles in collaborative school settings (e.g., Chrispeel, 1992; Firestone, 1996; Hart, 1995; Pounder, Ogawa, & Adams, 1995). Findings indicated that leadership in collaborative settings is necessarily expanded beyond the principal to involve numerous others, with emphasis on teachers and also parents. Also noted, however, were difficulties in determining how to share responsibilities and accountability. Crow (1998) emphasized that leadership in collaborative schools can be viewed as an influence relationship between teachers and principals; both are leaders and followers at different times. For example, teachers lead their peers and also influence the principal. "Understanding leadership as a relationship involves looking beyond formal authority as the source of leadership. Leaders may be formal authorities but may just as likely be those without formal authority" (Crow, 1998, p. 136). Principals and teachers must work together to create professional communities in which reflection and learning are embedded norms.

Lambert (1998) proposes a model for promoting leadership capacity in schools that intentionally focus on the development of teachers as leaders. Key assumptions for this model are as follows:

- Leadership [involves] reciprocal learning processes that enable participants to construct and negotiate meanings leading to a shared purpose of schooling.

- Leadership is about learning that leads to constructive change.

- Everyone has the potential and right to work as a leader.

- Leading is a shared endeavor, the foundation for the democratization of schools.

- Leadership requires the redistribution of power and authority. (Lambert, 1998, pp. 8-9)

Feiler, Heritage, and Gallimore (2000) also emphasize the role of teacher leaders for successful school improvement. "Improved teaching practices also require on-site expertise and leadership. Creating internal resources for reform increases the likelihood that curriculum and teaching improvements, from both internal and external sources, will become integrated, sustained qualities of a school's functioning" (Feiler et al., 2000, p. 66). They describe a model in which individual teachers are selected by the principal as in-house experts. Selection considerations included expertise in the area targeted for schoolwide improvement, leadership skills and potential, and respect among peers, with an emphasis on being viewed as a credible and valuable instructional resource. In this model, the teachers who functioned as instructional leaders were released one day each week to work directly with teachers. Activities included visiting and observing in classrooms, modeling instructional practices, and meeting with teachers to assist with planning and assessment. The authors emphasized the need to clarify the teacher-leader roles early in the process and to ensure that the principal continues support of the teacher leaders.

While remaining cognizant of the essential role of teachers as leaders in any successful school-improvement initiative, we cannot overemphasize the role of the principal. A multitude of studies points to the pivotal role of the principal in successful school improvement efforts (see, for example, Blase & Blase, 1999; Bryk et al., 1999; Klein-Kraut, 1993; Murphy, 1994; Prestine, 1993; Ronnenberg, 2000). They play critical roles in facilitating both teacher learning and teacher leadership. In a study of professional community in 248 elementary schools, for example, facilitative leadership by the principal was identified as a significant variable (Bryk et al., 1999). In particular, encouragement by principals for "teachers to be involved, to innovate, and to take risks" (p. 768) supported the presence of professional community.

Principals identified as effective instructional leaders intentionally promote reflection and collegial interaction among teachers, which is focused on teaching and learning. In an open-ended survey of over 800 teachers, Blase and Blase (1999) found that effective principals consistently engaged with teachers around instruction, encouraging them to be aware of and to continually reflect on their professional practice. They did this by making suggestions, providing feedback, modeling practices, using inquiry, soliciting advice and opinions, and giving praise. The principals in the Blase and Blase study also actively promoted the professional growth of teachers by emphasizing the study of teaching and learning, supporting collaboration and coaching relationships among teachers, encouraging and supporting the redesign of programs, applying the principles of adult learning to staff-development opportunities, and implementing action research to inform instructional decision making. The authors concluded by stating,

> Our data suggest that principals who are effective instructional leaders use a broad-based approach; they integrate reflection and growth to build a school culture of individual and shared critical examination for improvement. In doing so, they appear to embrace the challenges of growing and changing. . . . Above all, [they] talk openly and frequently with teachers about instruction. . . . (Blase & Blase, 1999, p. 371)

In another study focused on the role of principals as leaders of staff learning, Ronnenberg (2000) conducted a multisite case study to determine specific practices used by principals identified as effective instructional leaders. In other words, he was interested in what principals actually do to promote learning and leadership by staff members around instruction. He identified specific strategies, used by each of the principals, related to inspiring a shared vision, creating a positive culture with high expectations for staff and students, challenging existing practices, and promoting relationships with and among staff members. The principals intentionally fostered reflection and learning, with dialogue as a primary means for learning. Examples of specific practices that were identified (Ronnenberg, 2000) and that foster reflection and learning among staff members include

- Keeping the focus of staff learning on student achievement
- Aligning all staff members' learning activities on the shared vision of the school
- Scheduling time for collaborative team planning and dialogue, sometimes on a daily basis and intermittently for half- or full days
- Promoting study groups
- Conducting weekly brown-bag lunches focused on teaching and learning
- Encouraging group attendance at conferences to promote sharing and follow-up with colleagues
- Establishing a professional library

Principals also play a critical role in promoting leadership by teachers. Lambert (1998) asserts that the role of the principal is more important than ever and much more complex:

> It demands a more sophisticated set of skills and understandings than ever before. It is more difficult to build leadership capacity among colleagues than to tell colleagues what to do. It is more difficult to be full partners with other adults engaged in hard work than to evaluate and supervise subordinates. (Ronnenberg, 2000, p. 24)

She goes on to explain that "among the more important tasks for the principal is to establish collegial relationships in an environment that may previously have fostered dependency relationships" (pp. 24-25). This frequently involves intentionally redirecting requests for permission and for answers. Assumptions or assertions about the roles of the principal versus the roles of teachers also may need to be questioned if leadership is to be shared. "Principals can use authority to reinforce and maintain dependent relationships or to establish and maintain processes that improve the leadership capacity of the school" (p. 26). The questioning and responding strategies described in Chapter 2 (pages 27-30) can be used to promote inquiry and thinking on the part of teachers. This promotes the development of internal capacities and reduces the tendency to seek external answers and top-down direction. It is sometimes necessary for the principal to remain silent so that other perspectives will emerge. (Silence was described in Chapter 2 as a response strategy for promoting thinking.)

It is clear from both the literature and experience that as schools move toward more collaborative ways of operating, in which staff members' reflection and learning is an embedded norm, leadership must be shared by principals and teachers. Drath and Palus (1994, as cited in Schall, 1995) describe leadership capacities that pertain to anyone who steps forward to make sense of practice and lead others in doing so as well. According to Drath and Palus (1994, p. 23), leaders of practice must demonstrate

The capacity to understand oneself as both an individual and as a socially embedded being

The capacity to understand systems in general and as mutually related and interacting and continually changing

The capacity to take the perspective of another

The capacity to engage in dialogue

Schall (1995) emphasizes the advantage, if not necessity, of *swamp knowledge* (Schon, 1983; 1987) over technical-rational knowledge when it comes to leading forward movement in the world of practice.

Technical rationality and science are not particularly helpful here. Competence in the swamp is more a clinical matter. It derives less from applying scientific laws of behavior or technical models developed for the high hard ground and more from a deeper understanding of the situation at hand and its relationship to other similar situations. (p. 207)

Perhaps the most powerful influence that leaders, be they principals or teachers, can have on their colleagues is to model ongoing reflection and learning about practice. Schwahn and Spady (1998) describe authentic leaders as those who assume the role of lead learner in the organization. Authenticity is a characteristic of leaders that can compel even the most reluctant follower to consider learning and improvement.

Schoolwide Reflection: Examples From Practice

Making a commitment to use reflective practices on a schoolwide basis is both inspiring and courageous. It is inspiring because of all that is known about the challenges of creating and sustaining significant, meaningful changes in educational practice. To make such a commitment reflects an optimistic view of schooling, educators, and the potential for successful school change. Moving toward reflective practice at the schoolwide level is courageous because the territory is vast and mostly uncharted. Both the risks and potential are great. Progress can be difficult to determine, especially in the early, more vulnerable stages. In the two examples below, you will learn how and why reflection became a central capacity for educational improvement. In the first example, reflection emerged in the process of a mandated school-improvement initiative. In the second example, reflective practices emerged from a bottom-up, teacher-led initiative. Both examples span multiple years and offer a sense of the messiness involved in navigating schoolwide change and the need for a team of persistent, reflective educators to assume the roles of guide and facilitator of staff learning. Outcomes and key lessons learned about schoolwide reflective practices are presented at the end of each example.

Reflecting Back to Reflect Forward at Mountain View School

Mountain View School (pseudonym) is one of seven elementary schools in a suburban school district. It opened as a K-3 building with 250 students and added one grade level a year for 5 years, reaching its current K-8 grade span with 729 students. Several pivotal factors generated the need for staff reflection and dialogue:

(a) The district expected each school in the district to include faculty in the development of a 3-year building-improvement plan that recommended building renovations aligned with the mission, vision, and goals of the school; (b) many Mountain View staff members had expressed a need to revisit the school's original beliefs and practices now that the final grade had been added and growth had been stabilized; and (c) a core team of teachers who were involved in a project focused on promoting collaboration between general and special educators had identified schoolwide areas in need of faculty discussion and clarification. This example from practice is excerpted with permission from a full-length case study by Kronberg and Lunders (1997).

A lead team that included 12 teachers from Mountain View, 1 district staff-development coordinator, and 1 university-based partner designed and implemented a reflection and learning process that involved all staff members. The purpose was to reflect on and identify future action related to the guiding practices that were developed when Mountain View School opened 6 years earlier. Specifically, the process provided an opportunity for staff members to think again about the original guiding practices, to consider the continuation of these practices, to determine whether current practices aligned with the original guiding practices, and to identify appropriate future action. Following are the seven original guiding practices on which staff members reflected: multiage and flexible groupings; teacher-directed instructional teams; academic-enrichment, special-options program; self-directed, respectful learners; interdisciplinary, thematic learning experiences; K-8 school community; and environmental education and service learning.

In general, the flow of the reflection and dialogue process included (a) providing information to the entire staff in order to obtain both their understanding of and commitment to the process; (b) generating a focused dialogue in carefully constructed, small groups to obtain perspectives from all staff members (licensed and unlicensed personnel); (c) making sense of the information generated from the dialogue sessions; and (d) setting a direction for next steps. Overall, there was movement from reflection and dialogue to inquiry and action. This reflection and dialogue process was implemented in three phases: dialogue groups, educational plan groups, and inquiry-advisory teams. The entire process spanned a period of 18 months.

Dialogue Groups The first phase of the process involved all staff members in dialogue groups to engage in conversation about the seven guiding practices. All staff members had the opportunity to reflect and provide feedback about the guiding practices in three ways: individual reflection, journaling; small dialogue groups; and schoolwide dialogues, conversation (Figure 6.4). To prepare for the small-group dialogues, each staff member was provided with a journaling page (see Figure 6.5 on page 136) that connected to each practice. Related to some practices, an article was also provided. Most participants came to the dialogue groups with prepared notes on their journal pages. Five dialogue groups with about 15 members

Figure 6.4. Reflection Formats Used at Mountain View School

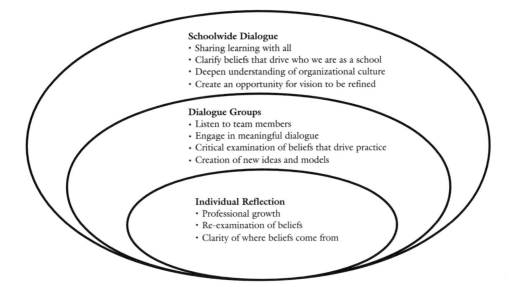

SOURCE: Reprinted by permission from Kronberg, R. K., & Lunders, C. (1997). "A Schoolwide Reflection and Dialogue Process at Mountain View School." In J. Montie, J. York-Barr, & R. Kronberg (Eds.), *Reflective Practice: Creating Capacities for School Improvement.* Minneapolis: University of Minnesota, Institute on Community Integration.

each (diverse representation) were formed. The agenda for addressing each practice area was sharing of general thoughts, articulating best-case scenarios, and articulating worst-case scenarios. Each dialogue group addressed four of the seven practices over the course of two meetings. In this way, each staff member had the opportunity to directly engage around four of the seven practices. For the remaining three, staff members were encouraged to share their journal entries.

Educational Plan Groups The second phase of the reflection and dialogue process involved the educational plan groups convening to make sense of the information generated in the dialogue groups and determine next steps. Educational plan groups were formed related to each of the seven practices. Staff members chose one or more guiding practices about which they would participate in an educational plan group. The groups convened and worked through a three-item agenda: what, so what, now what? More specifically, each group was charged with responsibility for: (a) identifying areas of agreement, disagreement, and confusion, based on the information generated in the dialogue groups; (b) listing recommendations; and (c) drafting a definition or description of the practice area. All the educational plan groups presented their work to the entire staff. Staff members were then provided with time to ask questions and to write and post comments on each presentation using Post-it notes.

Figure 6.5. Sample Journaling Page

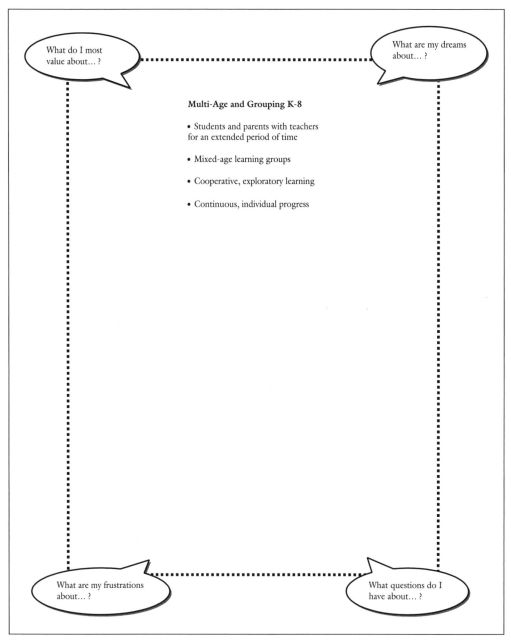

SOURCE: Reprinted by permission from Kronberg, R. K., & Lunders, C. (1997). "A Schoolwide Reflection and Dialogue Process at Mountain View School." In J. Montie, J. York-Barr, & R. Kronberg (Eds.), *Reflective Practice: Creating Capacities for School Improvement* (pp. 27-46). Minneapolis: University of Minnesota, Institute on Community Integration.

Inquiry and Advisory Teams In the final phase, inquiry-advisory teams were formed to further examine specific practice areas determined to be priorities by all staff members. All staff members were encouraged to participate in this phase of the process. Some were enthusiastic to continue the work initiated by the educational plan groups. Others chose not to participate on the teams. These teams met over the course of the following school year. Toward the end of that school year, recommendations were presented for approval by the staff. Approved recommendations set the course for future schoolwide action.

Outcomes and Key Learning Throughout the reflection and dialogue process, the majority of staff members articulated the importance of reconnecting around the practices at Mountain View School. New people who joined the staff over the years had missed earlier opportunities to engage in conversation about the school's mission, vision, and practices. The documents and plan that resulted from the process had meaning for most participants because they were involved in the process. Staff members felt valued to be included, believed it was important to discuss issues that were foundational to their schools, and appreciated hearing from staff members with whom they did not typically interact. Perhaps one of the most important outcomes was the strong foundation that was built for ongoing listening, inquiry, and action.

Reflection on the Mountain View dialogue process resulted in identifying several key learning factors:

- The importance of time for staff members to talk about important issues
- The struggle between spending time on that which feels urgent and that which feels important
- The benefits of participant diversity in small groups
- The use of written articles to prompt reflection and increase awareness of educational practices
- The active, visible, and ongoing involvement of the principal and assistant principal

The open-ended nature of the design and process was at times frustrating for members of the lead team. There was little doubt in their minds, however, that the end goals of clarifying who Mountain View School is and being part of shaping its future were worthy of the time and energy.

Inquiring Minds Unite at Urban High School

Urban High School (pseudonym) enrolls 2,000 students in a windowless building designed for 1,500 students. It has over 165 staff members, three major programs, and 16 departments. There have been six principals in the past 10 years. The teacher-led Inquiring Minds initiative began with a partnership between two teachers at Urban and two colleagues from a nearby university. These individuals shared an interest in creating a more collaborative work culture so that students with various learning challenges would be more successful academically and socially in this urban school. They also shared a set of beliefs that for a meaningful change to take hold at Urban, the process should be voluntary and emergent, meaning that staff members would be provided with the opportunity to engage in a learning process to figure out for themselves how to increase collaboration for student success. There were no other pressures on the school to participate in this improvement effort. The resources that were available included a university partner (averaging 10 to 20 hours a month of combined on-site and off-site time) and modest funding to pay for substitutes (used only during the first year). Described below is a sketch of the process, outcomes, and learning that spanned this 5-year development effort and continues today. (Readers interested in a full account are referred to the case study by Montie, York-Barr, Stevenson, & Vallejo, 1997).

Year 1: Reflect, Explore, and Focus

A series of meetings were held with staff members at Urban to explain the general purpose (increased collaboration for student success) and open-ended process (reflection and learning together to figure out what makes sense for moving forward) of the proposed initiative. The meetings were open to all staff members, and key teachers were specifically invited to attend. These key teachers included individuals who were respected as excellent student-centered teachers representing a variety of content and program areas in the school. Fourteen teachers stepped forward to participate.

During the first year, this group met eight times (ranging from 2 to 5 hours each meeting) to share perspectives about current realities at Urban, to study literature about collaboration and organizational learning, and to figure out whether or not and how to move forward. The conversations led to the realization that staff members did not know one another well, especially across grade levels and content areas, and that this resulted in fragmentation for students. The idea that more connections among teachers could create a better learning environment for students had taken on personal meaning for participants and was a source of inspiration.

The next step in the process, figuring out how to move forward, proved to be frustrating. The enormity of the task (promoting meaningful connections among teachers throughout the school), the uncertainty of what might be successful approaches, and a history of failed attempts at meaningful reform were unsettling. Would anyone else join in? Who has time to lead this effort? What could we do that might be successful? How can we know whether or not better communication improves student learning? Finally, participants decided to launch a schoolwide initiative during the next school year, focused on promoting reflective practices. Expanding the reflective capacities of teachers and providing opportunities for

Figure 6.6. Supporting Structures and Desired Outcomes for the Inquiring Minds Initiative at Urban High School

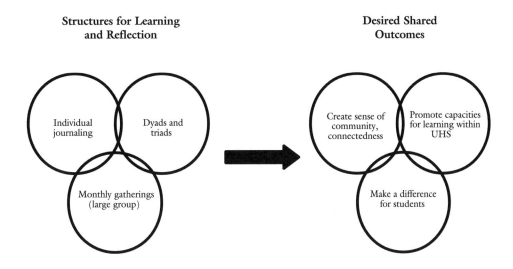

teachers to reflect and learn together about their instructional practices was viewed as one way to leverage the school's internal capacities to better serve students.

All staff members were invited to informal, informational sessions that were held during several lunch periods in the spring. Cake was served and the atmosphere was festive. The Inquiring Minds initiative was taking shape in the hearts and minds of teachers at Urban. They made plans to launch the learning process about reflective practices during a full-day retreat in August.

Year 2: Learning by Doing and Reflecting

A week before school started in the fall, about 25 Urban staff members, including the principal, attended the Inquiring Minds kickoff held in the lakeside meeting center of a nearby city park. There were four purposes of the kickoff: (a) to get to know one another and articulate desired outcomes of the Inquiring Minds process, (b) to engage in conversation about the meanings of reflective practice, (c) to introduce specific reflection strategies, and (d) to finalize a structure for learning together through a process of reflection. The structures to promote reflection and learning were individual journaling, weekly reflection on instructional practice in dyads or triads (self-organized), and monthly gatherings of the whole group at the lakeside meeting center (Figure 6.6). The shared, desired outcomes were expressed as making a difference for kids, promoting capacities for learning within Urban, and creating a sense of community and connectedness among staff members.

Of the three reflection structures, dyads and triads, and monthly gatherings were the two in which participants most consistently engaged. Individual journaling was dropped by most. An additional reflection structure, mailbox prompts, was introduced (described in Chapter 4). These written prompts were placed in participant mailboxes every couple of weeks. They contained humorous or contemplative passages, then outlined questions to prompt reflection about the passages or about participants' instructional practice. The lead team of two Urban teachers and two university partners designed and facilitated the monthly sessions, although all participants took turns leading the group in icebreaking activities and bringing refreshments and flowers or plants. Another significant support during the second year was a 2-day workshop held in the spring of the year that focused on strategies for promoting effective work as collaborative groups. Because of the relationships that had formed within the group and the reflection skills that were developed, Inquiring Minds participants quickly adopted the strategies presented in the workshop.

At the end of the year, a half-day gathering was held to reflect on the year, celebrate, and consider the group's future. Collegial relationships and reflective capacities among participants had increased. The Inquiring Minds group had taken on both personal and professional value. Directions for the following year were identified as continuing dyads and triads as well as the monthly gatherings, and expanding the effort by intentionally and consistently inviting others to participate. The potential of reflection to improve practice was experienced by the Inquiring Minds participants, and they were eager to include others.

Year 3: Inquiring Minds Sustains Through Transition

The third year was filled with unanticipated transitions and increased demands. A new team of administrators was assigned to Urban. Numerous school-improvement committees were mandated and pressing deadlines imposed. Many Inquiring Minds participants assumed leadership roles in these committees (usually in pairs) and attempted to make the committee processes meaningful. They viewed it as an opportunity to practice the reflection and collaborative group strategies learned the previous year. Their success was uneven. Participation in monthly gatherings fluctuated but served as a safe and supportive environment for the reflection and planning of the imposed committee work and for continuing efforts to meaningfully reflect on practice with colleagues (in dyads and triads). At the end of the year, several of the committees had shaped their work to include reflection and learning. The staff-development committee, for example, garnered support to pay for a 2-day, schoolwide kickoff for the following August. Over 50 staff members participated in this 2-day session focused on collaboration and emphasizing the critical role of reflection for staff learning and school improvement. This turnout indicated widespread interest in the topic and resulted in significant follow-through in a variety of staff-learning and school-improvement efforts.

Years 4 and 5: Embedding Reflection and Collaborative Norms Schoolwide

In the capable and determined hands of key teacher leaders, the Inquiring Minds initiative expanded and extended its influence during years 4 and 5. It expanded to include more people in dyads and triads and more people in monthly gatherings, which were relocated back at the building to promote ease of access. It extended to include use of the principles and strategies of reflection and collaboration in more than 12 varied work groups (e.g., committees, departments, child study). Recognizing the success of these groups, the principal asked Inquiring Minds participants to lead some of the more challenging (e.g., space committee) and important (e.g., mentoring) work groups.

Staff and Student Outcomes

What outcomes were realized from this multiyear, reflective practice initiative? Feedback from teachers throughout the Inquiring Minds initiative provided evidence of professional learning, improvement, and connection needs being met. Through the dyad-triad interactions, a safe opportunity had been provided to reflect on practice. Participants described feeling both supported and challenged in the presence of respected and caring colleagues. Furthermore, many of the teachers stepped forward to effectively serve in leadership roles, usually in pairs, for various school-improvement efforts. In these situations, a major objective was to create opportunities for meaningful learning and development in the context of mandated work groups. In regard to effects on students, many teachers identified specific improvements in practice that benefited students. They also felt that the strengthened and expanded relationships that had formed between teachers throughout the building created a safety net for students, especially for those students who were the initial focus of the Inquiring Minds process—the students who tend to fall through the cracks. In the words of one teacher, "If I do not know where to go for a student, I know someone who will know, or someone who will know someone who knows."

Learning From Inquiring Minds

Ten lessons are offered that can serve as guidelines for the design and facilitation of school-improvement efforts in which reflection and learning are foundational elements (Montie et al., 1997):

- Collaborative leadership by teams of teachers is a powerful force for meaningful school improvement.
- External partnerships add resources and help to maintain focus.

- The value of time to reflect and talk with colleagues cannot be overemphasized.

- Signs of hope and encouragement are needed to balance the inevitable ambiguities, uncertainties, and energy drains in the design and learning process.

- Relationships are a critical process and outcome.

- Efforts must be made to continually invite others into the process and expand the circle of participation.

- Honor openness in the process, allowing direction and meaning to emerge and reemerge from within the group.

- Clarify and revisit purpose, especially when learning and development get messy.

- Feel confident that the internal rewards of growth and learning—as teachers and for students—will sustain participation.

- There is no one, right way to start. Just do something thoughtful, and then reflect and adjust as you move forward.

The variables considered to be most significant in sustaining Inquiring Minds over time were the relationships that formed among participants (teachers throughout the school), the skills that developed to promote reflective practice, and, ultimately, the improvements in practice. These capacities, relationships, skills, and improvements, were the source of learning and energy that expanded and embedded reflection into a variety of educational practices at Urban High School. The enduring effects of this work continue to be recognized to date.

Schoolwide Reflection: More Ideas to Consider

Described below is a menu of ideas for promoting reflection throughout a school. The need to look within the school and its educators for untapped and underused capacities is emphasized. Also evident is the benefit that can be realized by introducing external knowledge (e.g., research literature) into the reflection process, to be thoughtfully considered by and adapted for implementation in the local school context.

Tapping the Community of Experts Within

A rural high school teacher, who was the staff-development coordinator, started a program called Community of Experts. He had noticed that many staff members attended external workshops to improve their skills. He wondered, Why not use the expertise already in his school and district? He recognized that sometimes outside consultants were needed to assist in developing specific skills, but he also knew educators could make better use of the knowledge, skills, and application inside their own districts.

To begin tapping the internal capacity in his own school district, he started by identifying specific areas of knowledge and expertise held by educators in the schools in his district. Second, he asked the staff members if they would be willing to share their knowledge and skills with their colleagues in the district. Third, he published a list of the existing expertise within the district for all district employees. Fourth, he organized a staff-development day and scheduled people to share their knowledge and skills. Last, he asked participants, What is needed next? Responses to this question produced ideas for the next staff-development day.

This staff-development coordinator honored the gifts and talents of those already in the system. In doing so, he strengthened a network of connections and resources among educators in his district.

Coaching Decreases Discipline Referrals

In a junior high school, a goal for the year was to reduce conflict, discipline referrals, and suspensions. As one way to support this goal, 25% of the certified staff was trained in coaching over the summer. This started conversations around questions, such as, How do we deal with students now, how do we want to deal with students, how can we solve discipline problems with the resources available, and how could we work as a team? In the fall of the year, another 25% of the staff was trained in coaching. In addition, the whole staff was offered a course on conflict management and classroom management, which was taught by the principal.

After the administrators, certified staff members, and noncertified staff members completed coaching courses, conversations about students became more inquiry oriented and focused on problem solving rather than on complaining and consequences. By the end of the year, data showed a reduction of discipline referrals by 30% and suspensions by 25%. Staff members also reported a reduction in conflicts with students and among staff members. To have achieved these outcomes required teamwork, conversations, and trust.

Learning in Faculty Meetings

The faculty meeting is one of the most renowned elements of school culture. Every year, educators log at least 50 hours in large-group faculty meetings. Over the course of a career, thousands of hours are probably captured in this forum. Recognizing that face-to-face time is one of the most valuable assets for staff learning, professionals have increasingly turned their attention to how to capture some of this time for learning. Killion (2000), for example, suggests how studying research about instructional strategies could be built into faculty meetings. At an initial meeting, staff members could generate a list of instructional strategies currently used, then work in small groups to identify when the strategy works well (e.g., types of curriculum, students, context) and when it does not. As a follow-up, staff members could then review research about the strategies and compare their use with uses suggested in the literature. At subsequent meetings, findings and implications from this review could be shared with faculty through posting on chart paper, for example. To accommodate this shift in emphasis during staff meetings, schools would need to use alternative ways to communicate some of the information that must be shared with all staff members. Suggestions include (Richardson, 1999): departmental, grade-level meetings; round-robin memos; electronic communication (e.g., e-mail, voice mail); newsletters and weekly bulletins; brown-bag lunches; copies of pertinent meeting minutes or reports; and bulletin-board messages in high-traffic areas.

At a minimum, beginning and ending meeting rituals can be used to instill a sense of connectedness around purpose. For example, make it regular practice to begin each faculty meeting by inviting staff members to share stories from practice, emphasizing either student or staff learning. Consider intentionally reviewing collaborative group norms, such as those presented in Chapter 5. Rituals emphasizing teamwork might be an effective way to close staff meetings, such as a group huddle and cheer, in the same way sports teams gather and cheer before assuming their field positions. Even though some of what necessarily occurs at staff meetings falls into the domain of management, opportunities can be created to reflect on the purpose and importance of teaching, to feel connected among a community of educators, and to learn with and from one another.

Schoolwide Study Groups

Increasingly emphasized is the use of study groups on a schoolwide basis when an organizational focus for learning has been identified. Murphy and Lick (1998) define a study group as "a small number of individuals joining together to increase their capacities through new learning for the benefit of students" (p. 4). A schoolwide study process might be launched to reflect on internal reasons for referral; to explore research about referrals and their link to academic and social behavior; and to identify appropriate intervention aimed at school and classroom context, curriculum, instruction, and interactions. "The power in the whole-faculty study-group process rests in the promise that teachers will become more knowledgeable and skillful at doing what will result in higher levels of student learning" (p. 5). Murphy and Lick (1988) offer a set of comprehensive strategies for developing whole-faculty study groups. For example, faculty may examine student data, including an analysis of disaggregated data (e.g., by gender and race), and determine that referrals for discipline and special education had steadily increased over the past 2 years. The next step is to study why this trend is occurring and options to intervene.

Francis, Hirsh, and Rowland (1994) describe how a school under pressure to reduce an achievement gap among students used whole-faculty study groups. During the first year, 10 study groups of six to eight teachers each were formed. Participation was mandated. All the groups read the same articles. During the second year, study groups were still mandated, but teachers could select their own group and topical focus of study. In the third year, mixed groups were once again intentionally formed, and the entire staff agreed on common topics. From this multiyear process, the authors concluded that vertical groups (e.g., heterogeneous groups of educators across grade levels) and common readings facilitated more connections and conversations throughout the school. Within groups, facilitators and ongoing communication and feedback were also important. Outcomes included increases in the knowledge base of teaching, professional dialogue, trust, classroom instruction, and staff morale. A professional code of conduct and a shared vision for the school also developed. Finally, conflict emerged and was viewed as positive and productive evidence that real change was happening.

Philosophy Club

A principal in a middle school started a Philosophy Club. Once a month, staff members were invited to join him at a local restaurant. He bought snacks, and staff members purchased their own beverages. The only requirement was that conversation had to be about learning, teaching, instruction, or anything else that would increase thinking and learning about educational practice. It was not permissible to complain, be negative, or talk about issues such as inadequate resources, unsupportive individuals, or excessive demands. Most of the time, conversation centered on an article about teaching and learning, a book someone was reading, a new strategy from a workshop, or a staff-development opportunity.

The number of staff members who showed up was very small at first, 5 or fewer. By the third month, the number was over 5, and by the sixth month, the group had grown to between 10 and 15 of the 35 staff members at the school. The principal shared that as a result of the Philosophy Club, staff members continued conversations at school that had started at the restaurant. In addition, conversations in the school became more focused on learning.

Sharing School History

As expressed by O'Neill (2000), "Organizations, like families, have historical memory, and historical memory is a part of an organization's culture" (p. 63). The stories that staff members hold and tell about their school have a powerful influence on what happens therein and, specifically, on how change is viewed. As with individuals, understanding the past of an organization can assist in predicting and planning for the future. A shared understanding of the past can also assist in bringing in new members. For example, one school begins the annual back-to-school staff retreat by passing a wand among teacher-elders, who share stories about the beginnings of the school and significant changes that have occurred throughout its history.

O'Neill (2000) describes a *historygram* process that provides an opportunity for staff members to review a school's past. A long sheet of shelf paper is mounted along the length of a wall, with a timeline running along the edge. The group is introduced to Neuhauser's (1988) tribal theory. Members are invited to depict specific eras of the school's history. They may also line up around the room, forming a human historygram. Members then write, and are invited to post, responses to the following questions (O'Neill, 2000, p. 64):

- What was the name of your era (for example, the crisis years)?
- What was the culture like? What tribal stories circulated? What symbols and ceremonies were important?
- What were the major initiatives?
- What were the goals of each initiative?
- How was the success of the initiatives measured? How did you know you were making progress? What was the basis for shifting direction?
- What values from the past do you want to bring into the future?

Shared responses offer an opportunity for reflection, analysis, and sense making. The historygram process can be used as a way of "orienting new members, reevaluating the group's purpose, creating a shared vision for the future, and helping members build commitment for a present initiative" (p. 64).

School Self-Review

Sutton (1995) describes a process for schools to conduct a self-review of teaching and learning centered around critical questions of purpose, instruction, and effectiveness. The following questions are suggested:

- Is teaching purposeful?
- Does our teaching create and sustain motivation?
- Does our teaching cater to the abilities and needs of all the pupils in the school or group?
- Are our lessons managed in ways that ensure an efficient and orderly approach to teaching and learning?

- Is there effective interaction between teacher and pupils?

- Is evaluation of pupils' progress used to support and encourage them and to extend and challenge them appropriately?

Related to each question, indicators are offered. Reflection on these questions and examination of respective indicators, compared with an articulated desirable future, provide the basis for a gap analysis of what is and what is desired. This creates a tension for planning action to move toward to the desired future state.

Getting Started
With Schoolwide Reflective Practice

Getting started with reflective practices at a schoolwide level is not a minor undertaking. To bolster your energy as you go, keep clearly in mind the ultimate potential of significant and sustained improvements in practice that result in higher levels of student learning. The greater the number and diversity of people involved, the greater the need for intentional design and ongoing support. A team of people is needed to guide the process. This team needs to understand the big-picture meaning of why reflection is a critical capacity for school improvement and how to facilitate learning and development at the organizational level. Members of this team must also model the value of reflection by continuing to reflect at the individual level, as well as within the lead team, throughout the development process. High levels of trust and commitment are needed. A lead team's commitment to one another, to the desired outcomes for students, and to the unfolding process keeps the initiative on the front burner. This is a significant factor because it is especially easy for proactive initiatives to fall by the wayside as urgent issues create pressure in the system.

To guide your thinking about moving forward with reflective practices at the schoolwide level, we offer the following questions, organized around four key elements in a design process: purpose (why?), people (who?), design and structure (what and how?), and outcomes (so what?). You may wish to choose just a few questions to begin a conversation with colleagues in your school.

Purpose . . . What and Why?

- Do important or pressing schoolwide issues create an opportunity to improve our reflection and inquiry capacities? Or are there a variety of important areas in which staff learning through reflection should be targeted?

- What do students identify as some of the greatest challenges or frustrations in our school? If student data were disaggregated by age, gender, race, or primary language, what would we learn about our effectiveness? What might be the implications of these findings?

- Looking schoolwide, what are major strengths related to student learning (e.g., program areas, teacher initiatives, personnel, support services)? In what areas are students experiencing the greatest challenges? How might reflection on our strengths and challenges offer insight about desired improvements in practice?

People . . . Who?

- If we were to take on a significant initiative, is the web of relationships in our building extensive enough and strong enough to move effectively toward implementation? How might we extend and strengthen the web of connections in a meaningful way?

- What is the level of trust in our building? How safe is it to have a conversation about instructional practice? How might trusting relationships be promoted?

- Who might lead and facilitate reflection and learning on a schoolwide basis? Who are the positive energy sources in the building? Who are the constructive bridge builders, the connectors?

- Who is highly respected and viewed as an instructional leader? How might the capacities of these individuals be tapped? What conversations might be held about promoting schoolwide reflection and learning?

- How will we continually promote the value of inclusivity? How will staff members be invited and encouraged to reflect and learn together? How will our learning about learning be shared among staff members?

Design and Structure . . . How?

- As a school community, where are we along the staff-learning continuum? How well is staff learning embedded into the daily and weekly schedule? What is our vision for continuous learning among staff members, and how close are we?

- What is the level of inquiry in our building? How skilled are our staff members in questioning, responding, and dialoguing in ways that promote thinking?

- What would be the effective ways for staff members to learn together? How might staff members form learning groups? Vertically? Horizontally? Mixing experienced and new teachers?

- What resources do we need to support our work? What internal capacities do we already have that could be tapped? What external capacities might be solicited?

- What's our plan for getting started? The goals and purpose? The outcomes or indicators? The general design and approach? The key individuals who will be involved? The skills or capacities that need to be developed or connected? The structures that allow reflection and learning together?

Outcomes . . . So What?

- What student learning outcomes are we focused on? Are we making progress toward these outcomes? How do we account for progress being made or not?

- How will we know whether reflection, learning, and improvement are taking hold? What evidence would we expect to observe, hear, or collect? How will we obtain and examine feedback about the progress we are making?

We invite you to use the Chapter Reflection: Capturing Your Thoughts form (Figure 6.7) on the next page to write down your thoughts in response to these questions. You may also wish to refer to Chapter 2 to be reminded of considerations for choosing meaningful topics on which to reflect, design options for staff learning, and personal capacities for promoting trusting relationships and thinking. In the next and final chapter, we present 10 lessons learned from our work of embedding reflective practices in the work of individual and school improvement. These lessons concisely capture a vision for reflective practice and may provide additional insight for the design and ongoing support of schoolwide reflective practice initiatives and efforts.

Figure 6.7. Chapter Reflection: Capturing Your Thoughts

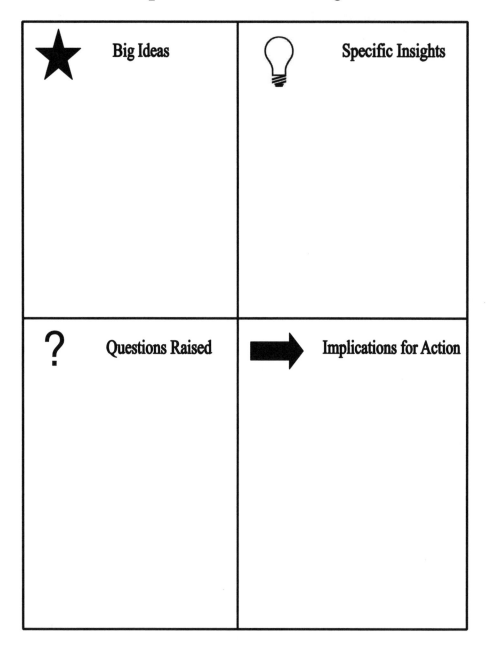

Moving Forward
With Reflective Practice

You must become the change you want to see in this world.
—Attributed to Mohandas Gandhi

To become the change you want to see in your world of practice means making a commitment to continuously learn and improve your practice. It means being a reflective practitioner. Begin with yourself; this becomes a fractal of the larger organization. Then, with others, expand reflective practices toward the outer level of the reflective practice spiral. Modeling is still the best teacher. "Organizations ultimately learn via their individual members" (Kim, 1993, p. 37). It is the collective reflection and learning, the establishment of a professional learning community, that hold the greatest potential for positively effecting student learning and lifelong learning capacities.

Wenger (1998) describes the rich learning opportunities available when individuals come together in a community of practice. She specifically emphasizes the strengths of a community in which members with varied degrees of experience intentionally choose to learn together across levels and areas of the organization. New members learn from and contribute to the culture of practice as they participate more fully in the community. Three key features in Wenger's depiction of communities of practice are mutual engagement, negotiated meaning through dialogue, and a shared repertoire to enhance the system—in other words, joining together, learning together, and then acting together.

As human beings, we have an internal drive for learning and growth. We are also social beings who naturally seek connections to others. Establishing communities of practice focused on learning is one way to satisfy these growth and social needs in addition to improving educational practice. A desirable future for our schools would be a program of attraction in which community members are drawn

in because of opportunities to learn, to connect with others, and to make a difference in the lives of children and families. Creating a program of attraction requires
intentionally developing the intellectual capacity of the school by promoting inquiry, seeking multiple perspectives on issues of practice, and examining both internal and external knowledge. It is likely that the school communities who are
most successful in establishing norms of reflection and continuous learning will be
rewarded with long-term, enthusiastic commitments by their staff. Wriston, as
quoted by Webber (1993), explains that "intellectual capital will go where it is
wanted and will stay where it is well treated" (n.p.). Reflective educators who are
committed to lifelong learning and improvement will be looking for a community
of practice that supports their values and commitments.

As stated in the preface to this book, we believe strongly in the positive intentions and strong commitments of today's educators. We also view educators as having knowledge and expertise that is largely untapped and underused. We know that
well-designed opportunities for reflection and learning together result in new insights about practice and new energy for teaching and learning. "Reflection is the
process that propels people along the journey from novice to expert. Not everyone
makes the whole journey; some people are stationary for many years . . ." (Butler,
1996, p. 270). A question to keep foremost in our minds is, How do we create
schools that are communities in which all members—students and adults—continue the journey of learning and continuous improvement? In this final chapter,
we share lessons learned about establishing reflective practices to promote learning
and improvement in schools. We also highlight some of the many paradoxes inherent in the ongoing design, implementation, and evolution of reflective practices.

Lessons Learned About Reflective Practice

Reflecting on our experiences of integrating reflective practices in schools, combined with our study of the literature, has led to the articulation of 10 important
lessons learned about this work. These lessons apply to a focus on reflective practice
at all levels in the reflective practice spiral. We offer these 10 lessons, using a R-E-F-
L-E-C-T-I-O-N mnemonic, in Figure 7.1.

R: Relationships are first. Establishing positive working relationships focused
on student learning is an essential foundation for reflective practice. Relationships
are the means by which information is communicated within a system. Relationships are the means for exploring who we are, what we believe, and how we should
act. Relationships are the building blocks for any system (Wheatley, 1992). Webber
(1993) advises that when you want to understand how an organization works, map
the relationship flow, not the formal organizational structure. Wheatley (1992)
writes, "The time I formerly spent on detailed planning and analyses, I now spend
looking at the structures that might facilitate relationships" (p. 36). How can a

Figure 7.1. Reflection Mnemonic for Lessons Learned About Reflective Practice to Improve Schools

Relationships are first

Expand options through dialogue

Focus on learning

Leadership accelerates reflective practice

Energy is required for any system to grow

Courage is needed to reflect and act

Trust takes time

Inside-out

Outside-in

Nurture people and ideas

web of interconnected relationships among staff members be woven throughout our school?

   E: Expand options through dialogue. Much knowledge about practice is inside the hearts and minds of educators. Conversations and dialogue are a way to "discover what they know, share it with their colleagues, and in the process create new knowledge for the organization" (Webber, 1993, p. 28). The value of time to talk together cannot be overemphasized. Through dialogue, understanding is increased, assumptions are made explicit, possibilities are explored, and options are expanded. Creative and divergent thoughts emerge as colleagues share their perspectives and interpretations about events, circumstances, and experiences. Creativity is one of our most valuable resources as education moves forward into the new millennium. An open exchange through dialogue allows community members to participate in the creative process of shaping future directions and moving forward with important work. Ownership, responsibility, and commitment increase. How can we get educators together to know one another, to remain open to other points of view, and to engage in dialogue that results in greater insights and expanded options for practice?

F: Focus on learning. The purpose of reflective practice is to increase learning for staff and students. If educators are not focused on learning, it is hard to imagine why students would be. At the core of reflective practice are the desire and commitment to continuously learn so that educational practice improves and all students learn at high levels. A focus on learning requires a certain amount of humility. It is an acknowledgement that we do not know everything. It requires giving up the need to be right. Ultimately, "enlightened trial and error outperforms the planning of flawless intellects" (Kelley as cited in Webber, 2000, p. 178). Reflection on practice involves learning through planning and reflective trial and error. Such learning is the way in which the process of teaching transforms events, experiences, and information into the tacit knowledge and wisdom of distinguished educators. The opportunities for learning to improve practice are limitless. How can we make learning become an explicit focus of conversations among staff members?

L: Leadership accelerates reflective practice. Leadership by the formal and informal leaders in a school is an essential organizational resource for reflective practice. Leadership must be shared among administrators and teachers. Without the principal, the commitment of resources and the commitment by people waivers. The beliefs, values, and actions of the principal influence strongly the alignment of staff members around reflection and learning. Without teacher leaders, the relationships that are essential for successful change will not be activated. The learning that emerges from the firsthand knowledge of students in the classroom context will not be part of the conversation. Teacher leaders understand the inner workings and relationships within a school and can access those relationships as resources to positively influence student learning. To support educators' learning, schools must be structured to encourage the intellectual stimulation that fosters continuous development (Stewart, 1997). It is the job of the leadership team to create the conditions necessary for fruitful conversations about practice to happen (Webber, 1993). How do formal and informal leaders work together to create an environment that promotes conversations about learning?

E: Energy is required for any system to grow. Living systems require energy to grow. Energy in schools emerges from people who are meaningfully engaged in the teaching and learning process. Reflection creates energy by leading to new discoveries and insights about practice. Reflection with others creates even more energy as discoveries and insights are shared and channeled among educators throughout the school. Without positive energy that is productively channeled, systems die.

Living systems cease to function when they do not have, or cannot make use of, the critical ingredients that create energy for life. Without educators who are reflecting and learning, schools will die. How can we tap and increase the positive energy that already exists in our school?

C: Courage is needed to reflect and act. Courage is the internal capacity that supports taking action, despite knowing the inherent risks. Making a commitment to reflective practice on a personal basis is a courageous act because it means opening ourselves up to considering multiple perspectives and ways of doing things. It means critically examining our assumptions and our behaviors. It means taking responsibility for our own learning and growth as professional educators and modeling this valued way of practice among our peers. Making a commitment to support reflective practice in groups or teams and throughout the school is a courageous act because it means going public with our commitments. It means being part of something that runs counterculture to the strong norms in schools of constantly doing rather than learning and doing. It means trying to walk the talk of reflective practitioners, holding ourselves accountable. How do we develop and sustain the courage it takes to critically examine our practice and to make our learning public?

T: Trust takes time. Trusting relationships are the foundation for learning together. In a trusting relationship, we allow ourselves to be vulnerable—a requisite for learning. We can be open to exploring our assumptions. We choose to take risks, confident that we will not be punished or embarrassed if we make mistakes. "Learning requires tolerating people who make mistakes. Learning requires inefficiency. Learning requires tolerating failure. Learning requires letting people try things that they've never done before, things that they probably won't be very good at the first time around" (Webber, 2000, p. 176). Fear, which is the opposite of trust, is way too prevalent in some schools today. Webber (2000) points out that everyone seems interested in organizational learning, but no one is much interested in allowing individuals to learn. Mistakes and inefficiencies are inevitably part of the learning process but too often are not gracefully accepted. Educators will not choose to learn, at least not publicly, unless they are in a safe environment. Trust is difficult to build and easy to destroy. How do we promote a high-trust learning environment in schools? How can we increase our own trustworthiness?

I: Inside-out. Becoming a reflective educator is a process of inside-out change. Reflection is an internal capacity that is tapped by a genuine desire to learn and grow, not by external mandates. In the words of Michael Fullan (1993), "You can't mandate what matters" (p. 125). What matters most for teaching and learning is what is in the hearts and minds of educators. It is this inner capacity that connects educators with children, and children with learning. Becoming a reflective educator involves figuring out our own identity—who we are as people, as teachers, and as learners. We can teach only who we are (Palmer, 1998). As we become more reflective, we can inspire an interest in others to become more reflective and to take the risks involved in continuously learning from and improving practice. Actions reflect beliefs and values. As Oliver Wendell Holmes reportedly said, "What you do speaks so loudly no one can hear what you are saying." How do we create the space in our lives to begin or to expand our commitment to reflective practice and personal change?

O: Outside-in. Becoming a reflective educator also requires being open to outside influences, such as colleagues with different views, findings from research, experiences of other schools and systems, and concerns expressed by the public and by policy makers. We must be willing to ask for input as well as to receive it. None of us is an island. We are influenced by our surrounding context and must pay attention to it. Sometimes, change happens only when forces from the outside press in. Everything is connected to everything else. Open systems that engage with the environment grow and evolve (Wheatley, 1992). If we ignore external influences, we do so at our own peril. Closed systems eventually devolve. This principle holds whether the system is a person, a partnership, a team, a school, a district, or a community. Reflection is a process for making sense of both internal and external influences and for determining priorities for action. How can we be continually aware of, and allow ourselves to be open to, our surrounding environment?

N: Nurture people and ideas. Be inclusive. Nurture creativity. Create a culture of attraction in which educators are drawn into a school community because their needs to learn, to create, and to make a difference in the lives of children are met. Nurture their creativity. Allow them to bring their unique contributions and gifts to the teaching and learning process. Teaching and learning make up a highly personal process. Effective educators vary greatly in their approaches and styles. For educators to bring their best to their work with children, they must be in places that nurture their growth, support their creativity, and offer feedback in the context of a trusting, professional learning community. Continue to invite people into the community of reflective educators. It is the collective energy that emerges from reflection and learning by many people that has the greatest potential for sustained and widespread improvement in educational practice. How can we be inclusive and nurturing of the many varied individuals in our school communities?

Paradox of Reflective Practice

Pathways to improvement in schools are less specific and more ambiguous than was once thought. The dynamic interplay among internal factors, combined with the influence of external factors, does not lend itself well to one prescription for improvement. The best we can do is to be guided by principles, not specific steps. Only the direction and design can be controlled, not the outcomes. And even the

Figure 7.2. Paradox of Reflective Practice

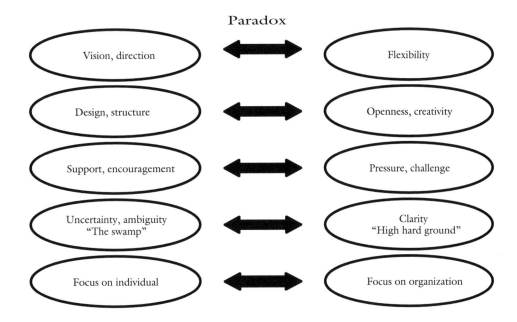

design must constantly evolve in response to given feedback, changing context variables, and new insights. Experimenting with reflective practice as one means of supporting school improvement has raised as many questions as answers about how to do this kind of work. Our understanding about paradox within reflective practice has been heightened. Paradox can be thought of as tension that exists around ideas that seem both contradictory and true at the same time. This is the nature of our world as a whole and also in education today. Areas of paradox that become evident in our reflection and analyses are shown in Figure 7.2.

For reflective practices to be initiated, there must be enough vision and direction for participants to know where the initiative is headed and why as well as enough flexibility to allow participants to shape the initiative and make it personally meaningful. There must be enough design and structure for the process to get underway as well as enough flexibility and creativity to allow ongoing adjustments that support an emergent learning process. There must be enough support and encouragement for participants to feel safe as well as enough pressure and challenge to promote divergent thinking. There must be acknowledgement of the uncertainty, ambiguity, and value of practice in the swamp as well as regard for the clarity of high-hard-ground knowledge reported in the research literature. There must be enough focus on individual learning and growth needs as well as attention to the learning and growth needs of the organization.

How much is enough? How do we discover the balance between the points? It's hard to tell until you get underway. What is important is to know that these areas of apparent contradiction are actually necessary tensions. Imagine launching a reflective practice initiative without any direction or aim. Why would anyone be compelled to participate? Imagine the presence only of support and encouragement, without pressure and challenge. How would new thinking emerge? Imagine a commitment to reflective practice without a design or structure to support it. How would you start? The nature of paradox is the coexistence of multiple and seemingly contradictory truths. The work of reflective practice rests solidly within both/and thinking instead of either/or thinking.

Closing

Embedding reflective practices in education is about creating significant cultural change in schools. It is messy. It can be complicated. There are no certain paths. The outcomes, however, can significantly and positively affect students. As you move through a process of becoming more reflective as an individual and with your colleagues, reflection-in-action, reflection-on-action, and reflection-for-action will provide the feedback needed to make adjustments. The Capturing Your Thoughts chapter-reflection page (Figure 7.3) can be used to write down ideas from this chapter that you may find useful for future reference as you continue your work in this area. Future practice and study about reflective practices for professional development and school improvement will increase our understanding about how to move forward. For now, congratulate yourself on beginning the process.

Feel confident that your choice to reflect on your practice will result in improvements for you and, most important, for the students in your school community. Remember that the objective is progress, not perfection. Keep clearly in mind:

> To reflect on action is to be a lifelong learner. To be reflective is a choice that is made against the background of beliefs and values. To be a constantly developing performer or to remain an expert performer requires the constant input of energy to do the work of reflection and learning. This energy source is inside the self; it is released by enabling understandings within the worldview. Quality performance is the outcome of a belief in quality. (Butler, 1996, p. 280)

What do you think you might do first as a result of reading this book? In what ways could you use this information tomorrow? Who else might work with you to expand reflection and learning in your school? If your school were a place in which students and staff continuously learn and have fun doing so, what would that look like? What would a desirable future school be like for you? How might you be part of that vision? How might you be part of making that vision a reality?

Figure 7.3. Chapter Reflection: Capturing Your Thoughts

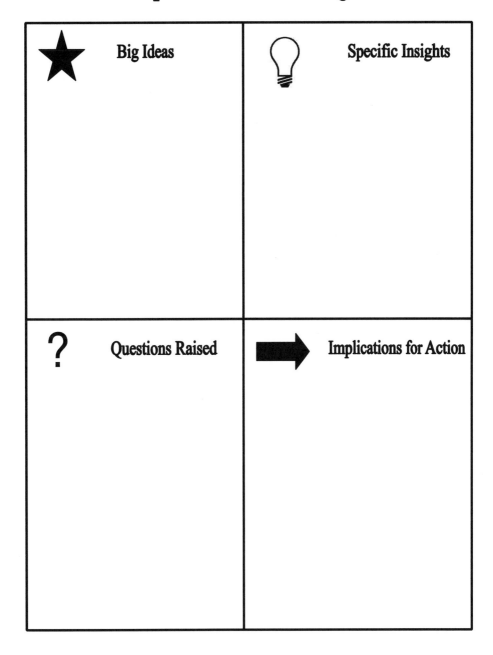

References

Adelman, N. (1998). *Trying to beat the clock: Uses of teacher professional time in three countries.* Washington, DC: Policy Studies Associates.

Ambrose, D. (1987). *Managing complex change.* Pittsburg, PA: Enterprise Group.

American Psychological Association. (1997). *Learner-centered principles: A framework for school redesign and reform.* Washington, DC: Author.

Argyris, C. (1977, September-October). Double loop learning in organizations. *Harvard Business Review,* 115-125.

Argyris, C., & Schon, D. (1974). *Theory in practice: Increasing professional effectiveness.* San Francisco: Jossey-Bass.

Arin-Krupp, J. (1991, October). *Motivating experienced school personnel.* Minneapolis, MN: Workshop presented by the Association for Supervision and Curriculum Development.

Arnold, G. C. S. (1995). Teacher dialogues: A constructivist model of staff development. *Journal of Staff Development, 16*(4), 34-38.

Bailey, K., Curtis, A., & Nunan, D. (1998). Undeniable insights: The collaborative use of three professional development practices. *TESOL Quarterly, 32*(3), 546-556.

Barnett, C. (1999). Cases. *Journal of Staff Development, 20*(3), 26-27.

Berliner, D. C. (1986, August-September). In pursuit of the expert pedagogue. *Educational Researcher,* 5-13.

Blase, J., & Blase, J. (1999). Principals' instructional leadership and teacher development: Teachers' perspectives. *Educational Administration Quarterly, 35*(3), 349-378.

Bohm, D. (1989). *On dialogue.* Ojai, CA.: David Bohm Seminars.

Brandt, R. (1998). *Powerful learning.* Alexandria, VA: Association for Supervision and Curriculum Development.

Bright, B. (1996). Reflecting on "reflective practice." *Studies in the Education of Adults, 28*(2), 162-184.

Brookfield, S. (1992). Why can't I get this right? Myths and realities in facilitating adult learning. *Adult Learning, 3*(6), 12-15.

Brown, J. D., & Wolfe-Quintero, K. (1997). Teacher portfolios for evaluation: A great idea or a waste of time? *Language Teacher, 21,* 28-30.

Brubacher, J. W., Case, C. W., & Reagan, T. G. (1994). *Being a reflective educator: How to build a culture of inquiry in the schools.* Thousand Oaks, CA: Corwin.

Bryk, A., Camburn, E., & Louis, K. S. (1999). Professional community in Chicago elementary schools: Facilitating factors and organizational consequences. *Educational Administration Quarterly, 35* (Suppl.), 751-781.

Butler, J. (1996). Professional development: Practice as text, reflection as process, and self as locus. *Australian Journal of Education, 40*(3), 265-283.

Caine, R. N., & Caine, G. (1997). *Education on the edge of possibility.* Alexandria, VA: Association for Supervision and Curriculum Development.

Calhoun, E. (1994). *How to use action research in the self-renewing school.* Alexandria, VA: Association for Supervision and Curriculum Development.

Canning, C. (1991). What teachers say about reflection. *Educational Leadership 48*(6), 18-21.

Carlson, R., & Bailey, J. (1997). *Slowing down to the speed of life: How to create a more peaceful, simpler life from the inside out.* San Francisco: HarperCollins.

Chrispeel, J. H. (1992). *Purposeful restructuring: Creating a culture for learning and achievement in elementary schools.* New York: Falmer.

Clarke, A. (1995). Professional development in practicum settings: Reflective practice under scrutiny. *Teaching and Teacher Education, 11*(3), 243-261.

Colton, A. B., & Sparks-Langer, G. M. (1993). A conceptual framework to guide the development of teacher reflection and decision making. *Journal of Teacher Education, 44*(1), 45-54.

Costa, A. L., & Garmston, R. (1988). *Cognitive coaching training manual.* El Dorado Hills, CA: Institute for Intelligent Behavior.

Costa, A. L., & Garmston, R. J. (1994). *Cognitive coaching: A foundation for renaissance schools.* Norwood, MA: Christopher-Gordon.

Costa, A. L., & Kallick, B. (2000a). *Activating and engaging habits of mind.* Alexandria, VA: Association for Supervision and Curriculum Development.

Costa, A. L., & Kallick, B. (2000b). Getting into the habit of reflection. *Educational Leadership, 57*(7), 60-62.

Covey, S. (1989). *The seven habits of highly effective people.* New York: Fireside.

Cranton, P. (1996). Types of group learning. In S. Imel (Ed.), Learning in groups: Exploring fundamental principles, new uses, and emerging opportunities. *New Directions for Adult and Continuing Education, 71.* San Francisco: Jossey-Bass.

Crow, G. M. (1998). Implications for leadership in collaborative schools. In D. G. Pounder (Ed.), *Restructuring schools for collaboration: Promises and pitfalls* (pp. 135-153). Albany: State University of New York.

de Bono, E. (1970). *Lateral thinking.* New York: Harper & Row.

Deci, E. L. (1995). *Why we do what we do.* New York: Grosset Putnam.

Dewey, J. (1933). *How we think.* Boston: D. C. Heath.

Dewey, J. (1938). *Experience and education* (6th ed.). New York: Macmillan.

Dietz, M. E. (1999). Portfolios. *Journal of Staff Development, 20*(3), 45-46.

Diss, R. E., Buckley, P. K., & Pfau, N. D. (1992). Interactive reflective teaching: A school-college collaborative model for professional development. *Journal of Staff Development, 13*(2), 28-31.

Donahoe, T. (1993, December). Finding the way: Structure, time, and culture in school improvement. *Phi Delta Kappan, 75*(3), 298-305.

Drath, W. H., & Palus, C. J. (1994). *Making common sense: Leadership as meaning-making in a community of practice*. Greensboro, NC: Center for Creative Leadership.

Easton, L. B. (1999). Tuning protocols. *Journal of Staff Development, 20*(3), 54-55.

Ellinor, L., & Gerard, G. (1998). *Dialogue: Rediscovering the transforming power of conversation*. New York: John Wiley.

Eraut, J. (1985). Knowledge creation and knowledge use in professional contexts. *Studies in Higher Education, 10*(2), 117-133.

Even, M. (1987). Why adults learn in different ways. *Lifelong Learning: An Omnibus of Practice and Research, 10*(8), 22-25, 27.

Feiler, R., Heritage, M., & Gallimore, R. (2000). Teachers leading teachers. *Educational Leadership, 57*(8), 66-69.

Firestone, W. A. (1996). Leadership: Roles of functions? In K. Leithwood et al. (Eds.), *International handbook of educational leadership and administration*. London: Kluwer.

Francis, S., Hirsh, S., & Rowland, C. (1994). Improving school culture through study groups. *Journal of Staff Development, 15*(2), 12-15.

Frankl, V. (1959). *Man's search for meaning*. Boston: Beacon.

Fullan, M. G. (1993). Why teachers must become change agents. *Educational Leadership, 50*(6), 12-17.

Fullan, M. G. (2000a). The return of large scale reform. *Journal of Educational Change, 1,* 5-8.

Fullan, M. G. (2000b). The three stories of education reform. *Phi Delta Kappan, 81*(8), 581-584.

Fullan, M. G., & Stiegelbauer, S. M. (1991). *The new meaning of educational change* (2nd ed.). New York: Teachers College Press.

Garmston, R., & Wellman, B. (1995). Adaptive schools in a quantum universe. *Educational Leadership, 52*(7), 6-12.

Garmston, R., & Wellman, B. (1997). *The adaptive school: Developing and facilitating collaborative groups*. El Dorado Hills, CA: Four Hats.

Garmston, R., & Wellman, B. (1999). *The adaptive school: A sourcebook for developing collaborative groups*. Norwood, MA: Christopher-Gordon.

Gitlin, A. (1999). Collaboration and progressive school reform. *Educational Policy, 13*(5), 630-658.

Glanz, J. (1998). *Action research: An educational leader's guide to school improvement*. Norwood, MA: Christopher-Gordon.

Glanz, J. (1999). Action research. *Journal of Staff Development, 20*(3), 22-23.

Glickman, C. D. (1988). Knowledge and uncertainty in supervision of instruction. In P. P. Grimmet & G. L. Erickson (Eds.), *Reflection in teacher education* (pp. 57-66). New York: Teachers College Press.

Glickman, C. D. (1995). *Action research: Inquiry, reflection, and decision making* [Video 4-95037]. Alexandria, VA: Association for Supervision and Curriculum Development.

Goldberg, M. (1998). *The art of the question.* New York: John Wiley.

Goldberg, S. M., & Pekso, E. (2000). The teacher book club. *Educational Leadership, 57*(8), 39-41.

Goldman, D. (1995). *Emotional intelligence: Why it can matter more than IQ.* New York: Bantam.

Grimmet, P. P., MacKinnon, A. M., Erickson, G. L., & Riecken, T. J. (1990). Reflective practice in teacher education. In R. T. Clift, W. R. Houston, & M. C. Pugach (Eds.), *Encouraging reflective practice in education: An analysis of issues and programs* (pp. 20-38). New York: Teachers College Press.

Grinder, M. (1993). ENVOY: Your personal guide to classroom management. Battle Ground, WA: Michael Grinder & Associates Training.

Hackman, R. J. (1991). *Groups that work and those that don't: Creating conditions for effective teamwork.* San Francisco: Jossey-Bass.

Hagstrom, D., Hubbard, R., Hurtig, C., Mortola, P., Ostrow, J., & White, V. (2000). Teaching is like . . . ? *Educational Leadership, 57*(8), 24-27.

Hare, A. P. (1994). *Small group research: A handbook.* Greenwich, CT: Ablex.

Harri-Augstein, S., & Thomas, L. (1991). *Learning conversations.* London: Routledge.

Hart, A. W. (1995). Reconceiving school leadership: Emergent views. *Elementary School Journal, 96,* 9-28.

Harwell-McKee, K. (1999). Coaching. *Journal of Staff Development, 20*(3), 28-29.

Hatton, N., & Smith, D. (1995). Reflection in teacher education: Towards definition and implementation. *Teaching and Teacher Education, 11*(1), 33-49.

Hawley, W. D., & Valli, L. (2000, August). Learner centered professional development. *Phi Delta Kappa Research Bulletin, 27,* 7-10.

Henry, S. K., Scott, J. A., Wells, J., Skobel, B., Jones, A., Cross, S., Butler, C., & Blackstone, T. (1999). Linking university and teacher community: A "think tank" model of professional development. *Teacher Education and Special Education, 22*(4), 251-268.

Hord, S. (1997). *Professional learning communities: Communities of continuous inquiry and improvement.* Austin, TX: Southwest Educational Development Laboratory.

Hord, S. M., Rutherford, W. L., Huling-Austin, L., & Hall, G. E. (1987). *Taking charge of change.* Alexandria, VA: Association for Supervision and Curriculum Development.

Horsley, D. L., & Loucks-Horsley, S. (1998). CBAM brings order to the tornado of change. *Journal of Staff Development, 19*(4), 17-20.

Huberman, M. (1992). Critical introduction. In M. Fullan (Ed.), *Successful school improvement*. Milton Keynes: Open University Press.

Isaacs, W. (1999). *Dialogue and the art of thinking together*. New York: Currency.

Johnson, D. W., & Johnson, R. T. (1999). *Learning together and alone: Cooperative, competitive, and individualistic learning* (5th ed.). Needham Heights, MA: Allyn & Bacon.

Johnston, M. (1994). Contrasts and similarities in case studies of teacher reflection and change. *Curriculum Inquiry, 24*(1), 9-26.

Kahn, W. A. (1992). To be fully there: Psychological presence at work. *Human Relations, 45*(4), 321-349.

Keating, C. N. (1993). Promoting growth through dialogue journals. In G. Wells (Ed.), *Changing schools from within: Creating communities of inquiry* (pp. 217-236). Toronto, Canada: Ontario Institute for Studies in Education.

Killion, J. (1999). Journaling. *Journal of Staff Development, 20*(3), 36-37.

Killion, J. (2000, March). Explore research to identify best instructional strategies. *Results*, 3.

Killion, J., & Todnem, G. (1991). A process of personal theory building. *Educational Leadership, 48*(6), 14-17.

Killion, J. P., & Simmons, L. A. (1992). The Zen of facilitation. *Journal of Staff Development, 13*(3), 2-5.

Kim, D. (1993, Fall). The link between individual and organizational learning. *Sloan Management Review*, 37-50.

King, M. B., & Newmann, F. M. (2000). Will teaching learning advance school goals? *Phi Delta Kappan, 81*(8), 576-580.

Klein-Kracht, P. A. (1993, July). The principal in a community of learning. *Journal of School Leadership, 3*(4), 391-399.

Knoster, T. P., Villa, R. A., & Thousand, J. S. (2000). A framework for thinking about systems change. In R. A. Villa & J. S. Thousand (Eds.), *Restructuring for caring and effective education* (2nd ed., pp. 93-128). Baltimore: Paul H. Brookes.

Kohn, A. (1993). *Punished by rewards: The trouble with gold stars, incentive plans, A's, praise, and other bribes*. New York: Houghton Mifflin.

Kronberg, R., & Lunders, C. (1997). A school-wide reflection and dialogue process at Mountain View School. In J. Montie, J. York-Barr, & R. Kronberg (Eds.), *Reflective practice: Creating capacities for school improvement* (pp. 27-45). Minneapolis, MN: University of Minnesota, Institute on Community Integration.

Kruse, S. D., Louis, K. S., & Bryk, A. (1995). An emerging framework for analyzing school-based professional community. In K. S. Louis & S. D. Kruse (Eds.), *Professionalism and community: Perspectives on reforming urban schools* (pp. 23-42). Thousand Oaks, CA: Corwin.

Lambert, L. (1998). *Building leadership capacity in schools*. Alexandria, VA: Association for Supervision and Curriculum Development.

Lame Deer, J., & Erdoes, R. (1994). *Lame Deer seeker of visions*. New York: Washington Square.

Langer, G. M., & Colton, A. B. (1994). Reflective decision-making: The cornerstone of school reform. *Journal of Staff Development, 15*(1), 2-7.

Lasley, T. J. (1992). Promoting teacher reflection. *Journal of Staff Development, 13*(1), 24-29.

Leat, D. (1995). The costs of reflection in initial teacher education. [Cambridge, UK] *Journal of Education, 25*(2), 161-174.

Lee, P. (1995). *Creating collaborative work cultures: Effective communication*. Drake, CO: Changing Points of View.

Lerner, P. (1997). *Collaborative action research: Study guide*. Santa Monica, CA: Canter Educational Productions.

Levin, B. B. (1995) Using the case method in teacher education: The role of discussion and experience in teachers' thinking about cases. *Teaching and Teacher Education, 11*(1), 63-79.

Lieberman, A., & Miller, L. (1999). *Teachers transforming their world and their work*. New York: Teachers College Press.

Louis, K. S. (1992). Restructuring and the problem of teachers' work. In A. Lieberman (Ed.), *The changing contexts of teaching: 91st yearbook of the National Society for the Study of Education*, (Vol. 1, pp. 138-156). Chicago: University of Chicago Press.

Louis, K. S., & Kruse, S. D. (Eds.). (1995). *Professionalism and community: Perspectives on reforming urban schools*. Thousand Oaks, CA: Corwin.

Magestro, P. V., & Stanford-Blair, N. (2000). A tool for meaningful staff development. *Educational Leadership, 57*(8), 34-35.

Marks, H., & Louis, K. S. (1999, December). Teacher empowerment and the capacity for organizational learning. *Educational Administration Quarterly, 35*, (Suppl.), 707-750.

McGregor, G., Halvorsen, A., Fisher, D., Pumpian, I., Bhaerman, B., & Salisbury, C. (1998). Professional development for all personnel in inclusive schools. *Consortium on Inclusive Schooling Practices Issue Brief, 3*(3). Retrieved January 10, 2000, from the Allegheny University of the Health Sciences Child and Family Studies Program on the World Wide Web: www.asri.edu/CFSP/brochure/prodevib.htm

McLean, J. E. (1995). *Improving education through action research: A guide for administrators and teachers*. Thousand Oaks, CA: Corwin.

Merriam, S. B. (1993). *An update on adult learning theory*. San Francisco: Jossey-Bass.

Mitchell, R. (1999). Examining student work. *Journal of Staff Development, 20*(3), 32-33.

Moller, G., & Katzenmeyer, M. (1996). The promise of teacher leadership. *New Directions for School Leadership, 1*(1), 1-17.

Montie, J., York-Barr, J., Stevenson, J., & Vallejo, B. (1997). Inquiring minds unite at urban high school. In J. Montie, J. York-Barr, & R. Kronberg (Eds.),

Reflective practice: Creating capacities to improve schools (pp. 49-76). Minneapolis: University of Minnesota, Institute on Community Integration.

Moore, M., & Gergen, P. (1989). *Managing risk taking during organizational change.* King of Prussia, PA: Organization Design and Development.

Murphy, C., & Lick, D. W. (1998). *Whole faculty study groups: A powerful way to change schools and enhance learning.* Thousand Oaks, CA: Corwin.

Murphy, J. (1994). Transformational change and the evolving role of the principal: Early empirical evidence. In J. Murphy & K. Seashore-Louis (Eds.), *Reshaping the principalship: Insights from transformational reform effort* (pp. 20-53). Thousand Oaks, CA: Corwin.

Neuhauser, P. C. (1988). *Tribal warfare in organizations.* New York: Harper Business.

Newmann, F., & Wehlage, G. (1995). Successful school restructuring. Madison: University of Wisconsin, Center on Organization and Restructuring of Schools.

Nhat Hanh, T. (1993). *Interbeing: Fourteen guidelines for engaged Buddhism.* Berkeley: Parallax.

Nichol, L. (Ed.). (1996). *On dialogue.* New York: Routledge.

North Central Regional Educational Laboratory. (1994). Professional development: Changing times. *Policy Briefs, Reports, 4,* 1-6.

O'Neill, J. (2000). Capturing an organization's oral history. *Educational Leadership, 57*(8), 63-65.

Osterman, K. F., & Kottkamp, R. B. (1993). *Reflective practice for educators: Improving schooling through professional development.* Newbury Park, CA: Corwin.

Palmer, P. (1998). *The courage to teach.* San Francisco: Jossey-Bass.

Parades-Scribner, J. (1999). Professional development: Untangling the influence of work context on teacher learning. *Educational Administration Quarterly, 35*(2), 238-266.

Perkins, D. (1992). *Smart schools.* New York: Free Press.

Pounder, D. G. (1999). Teacher teams: Exploring job characteristics and work-related outcomes of work group enhancement. *Educational Administration Quarterly, 35*(3), 317-348.

Pounder, D. G., Ogawa, R. T., & Adams, E. A. (1995). Leadership as an organization-wide phenomena: Its impact on school performance. *Educational Administration Quarterly, 31*(4), 564-588.

Powerful designs for learning. (1999, Summer). *Journal of Staff Development, 20*(3).

Prestine, N. A. (1993, July). Extending the essential schools metaphor: Principal as enabler. *Journal of School Leadership, 3*(4), 356-379.

Pugach, M. C., & Johnson, L. J. (1990). Developing reflective practice through structured dialogue. In R. T. Clift, W. R. Houston, & M. C. Pugach (Eds.), *Encouraging reflective practice in education: An analysis of issues and programs* (pp. 186-207). New York: Teachers College Press.

Pugh, S. L., Hicks, J. W., Davis, M., & Venstra, T. (1992). *Bridging: A teacher's guide to metaphorical thinking.* Urbana, IL: National Council of Teachers of English.

Ramsden, P. (1992). *Learning to teach in higher education*. London: Routledge.

Rapaport, D. (1999). Cadres. *Journal of Staff Development, 20*(3), 24-25.

Raywid, M. (1993). Finding time for collaboration. *Educational Leadership, 51,* 30-34.

Rich, S. (1992). Teacher supports groups: Providing a forum for professional development. *Journal of Staff Development, 13*(3), 32-35.

Richards, J. C., & Lockhart, C. (1994). *Reflective teaching in second language classrooms*. Cambridge, UK: Cambridge University Press.

Richardson, J. (1997). Putting student learning first put these schools ahead. *Journal of Staff Development, 18*(2), 42-47.

Richardson, J. (1998). We're all here to learn. *Journal of Staff Development, 19*(4), 49-55.

Richardson, J. (1999, October-November). Harness the potential of staff meetings. *Tools for Schools,* 1-3. Oxford, OH: National Staff Development Council.

Robbins, P. (1999). Mentoring. *Journal of Staff Development, 20*(3), 40-42.

Rogers, C. (1986). Carl Rogers on the development of the person-centered approach. *Person-Centered Review, 1*(3), 257-259.

Ronneberg, S. C. (2000). *The urban school leader as change agent: Case studies of three urban school principals*. Unpublished doctoral dissertation, University of Minnesota, Minneapolis.

Rosenholtz, S. J. (1989). *Teachers' workplace: The social organization of schools*. New York: Longman.

Ross, D. D. (1989, March-April). First steps in developing a reflective approach. *Journal of Teacher Education,* 22-30.

Ross, D. D. (1990). Programmatic structures for the preparation of reflective teachers. In R. T. Clift, W. R. Houston, & M. C. Pugach (Eds.), *Encouraging reflective practice in education: An analysis of issues and programs* (pp. 97-118). New York: Teachers College Press.

Sagor, R. (1992). *How to conduct collaborative action research*. Alexandria, VA: Association for Supervision and Curriculum Development.

Sagor, R. (2000). *Guiding school improvement with action research*. Alexandria, VA: Association for Supervision and Curriculum Development.

Schall, E. (1995). Learning to love the swamp: Reshaping education for public service. *Journal of Policy Analysis and Management, 14*(2), 202-220.

Schein, E. (1992). *Organizational culture and leadership*. San Francisco: Jossey-Bass.

Schon, D. A. (1983). *The reflective practitioner: How professionals think in action*. New York: Basic Books.

Schon, D. A. (1987). *Educating the reflective practitioner: Toward a new design for teaching and learning in the professions*. San Francisco: Jossey-Bass.

Schwahn, C. J., & Spady, W. G. (1998). *Total leaders*. Arlington, VA: American Association for School Administrators.

Sherin, M. G. (2000). Viewing teaching on videotape. *Educational Leadership, 57*(8), 36-38.

Smyth, J. (1989). Developing and sustaining critical reflection in teacher education. *Journal of Teacher Education, 40*(2), 2-9.

Sommers, W. A. (August 4, 1995). *Thinking is a consequence of questions.* Minneapolis, MN: Cognitive coaching seminar presented at St. Mary's Greek Orthodox Church.

Sparks-Langer, G. M., & Colton, A. (1991). Synthesis of research on teachers' reflective thinking. *Educational Leadership, 48*(6), 37-44.

Sparks-Langer, G. M., Simmons, J. M., Pasch, M., Colton, A., & Starko, A. (1990). Reflective pedagogical thinking: How can we promote it and measure it? *Journal of Teacher Education, 41*(4), 23-32.

Steffy, B. E., Wolfe, M. P., Pasch, S. H., & Enz, B. J. (2000). *Life cycle of the career teacher.* Thousand Oaks, CA: Corwin.

Stewart, T. A. (1997). *Intellectual capital.* New York: Doubleday-Currency.

Stringer, E. T. (1996). *Action research : A handbook for practitioners.* Thousand Oaks, CA: Sage.

Sutton, R. (1995). *School self review.* Salford, UK: RS Publications.

Taggart, G. L., & Wilson, A. P. (1998). *Promoting reflective thinking in teachers: 44 Action strategies.* Thousand Oaks, CA: Corwin.

Thousand, J. S., & Villa, R. (2000). Collaborative teams: Powerful tools for school restructuring. In R. Villa & J. S. Thousand (Eds.), *Restructuring for caring and effective education* (2nd ed., pp. 254-291). Baltimore: Paul H. Brookes.

Towery, T. (1995). *The wisdom of wolves.* Franklin, TN: Wessex.

Tuckman, B. W. (1965). Developmental sequence in small groups. *Psychological Bulletin, 63*, 384-399.

U.S. Department of Education (1996). *Breaking the tyranny of time: Voices from the Goals 2000 Teacher Forum.* Washington, DC: Government Printing Office.

Van Manen, V. (1977). Linking ways of knowing with ways of being practical. *Curriculum Inquiry, 6*(3), 205-228.

Vaughan, J. C. (1990). Foreword. In R. T. Clift, W. R. Houston, & M. C. Pugach (Eds.), *Encouraging reflective practice in education: An analysis of issues and programs* (pp. vii-xi). New York: Teachers College Press.

Vella, J. (1994). *Learning to listen, learning to teach: The power of dialogue in educating adults.* San Francisco: Jossey-Bass.

Villa, R. A., & Thousand, J. S. (1992). Restructuring public school systems: Strategies for organizational change and progress. In R. A. Villa, J. S. Thousand, W. Stainback, & S. Stainback (Eds.), *Restructuring for caring and effective education: An administrative guide to creating heterogeneous schools,* (109-138). Baltimore: Paul H. Brookes.

Wallace, M. J. (1979). *Microteaching and the teaching of English as a second or foreign language in teacher training institutions.* Edinburgh, Scotland: Moray House College of Education, Scottish Centre of Education Overseas.

Watts, G. D., & Castle, S. (1993, December). Reform of and as professional development. *Phi Delta Kappan, 75*(3), 306-310.

Webb, G. (1995). Reflective practice, staff development and understanding. *Studies in Continuing Education, 17*(1 & 2), 70-77.

Webber, A. M. (1993, January-February). What's so new about the new economy? *Harvard Business Review,* 24-42.

Webber, A. M. (2000, June). Why can't we get anything done? *Fast Company, 35,* 168-170, 176-180.

Wenger, E. (1998). *Communities of practice.* Cambridge, UK: Cambridge University Press.

Wheatley, M. (1992). *Leadership and the new science.* San Francisco: Berrett-Kohler.

Will, A. M. (1997, Winter). Group learning in workshops. *New Directions for Adult and Continuing Education, 76,* 33-40.

Wilson, B. L., & Corbett, H. D. (1999). Shadowing students. *Journal of Staff Development, 20*(3), 47-48.

Wolfe, P. (1997, December). *Brain theory applications to the classroom.* Preconference workshop presented at the National Staff Development Council, Nashville, TN.

York-Barr, J., Kronberg, R., & Doyle, M. B. (1996). *Creating inclusive school communities. Module 4: Collaboration: Redefining roles, practices, and structures.* Baltimore: Paul H. Brookes.

Zeichner, K. M. (1993). Connecting genuine teacher development to the struggle for social justice. *Journal of Education for Teaching, 19*(1), 5-20.

Zeichner, K. M., & Liston, D. P. (1987). Teaching student teachers to reflect. *Harvard Educational Review, 57,* 23-48.

Zeichner, K. M., & Liston, D. P. (1996). *Reflective teaching: An introduction.* Mahwah, NJ: Lawrence Erlbaum.